Random Samplings: The Group Show 2017

April 7-May 27, 2017

Black Heritage Gallery
809 Kirby Street, Ste. 207
The Central School of Arts
&
Humanities Center
Lake Charles, Louisiana 70601

Catalog Design: www.salongosart.com

Author: Sálongo Lee

Published By www.createspace.com An Amazon.com Company

ISBN: 13: 978-1544685007

Black Heritage Gallery

The gallery, a project of Black Heritage Festival of Louisiana, Inc, opened on June 28, 2001 with a grant from the Junior League of Lake Charles, Inc. In February 2008, Lt. Governor Mitch Landrieu announced the gallery as one of the 26 initial sites on Louisiana's African-American Trail. A vision of Stella Miller and Frankie Lane.

THE GALLERY IS THE ONLY ARTS AND CULTURAL INSTITUTION OF ITS KIND IN SOUTHWEST LOUISIANA.

If you are interested in showcasing your art, being placed on the mailing list, volunteering or just need information, please email us at blackheritagegallery@gmail.com.

Judith Washington, Executive Director
Stella Miller, Curator
Deborah, LaFleur, Assistant

Paul Picheloup and Derrick Guidry, Design & Installation

www.bhflc.org | 337.488.0567
Gallery Hours: M-F 9:00AM to 5:00PM & Saturday by Appointment

The Artists:

Ron Chapman

Stained Glass & Paintings

Frank Jackson

B&W Photography

Randell Henry

Abstract Paintings

George Larkins, II

B&W Photography

Sálongo Lee

Color Photography on Canvas

Gregory Robinson, Jr.

Paintings & Wood Burning

MonaLisa Whitaker

Photography

Ron Witherspoon

B&W Photography

Katelynn Yvon

Paintings

From The Curator

I believe in every artist there is a curator waiting for that chance to organize an exhibition. I have been fortunate over the years to have had the opportunities to exhibit my work as a visual artist across the nation, and to organize and produce exhibitions of emerging and mid career visual artists from across the country.

This exhibition "Random Samplings: The Group Show 2017" is the second exhibition at Black Heritage Gallery that has allowed me to bring together a diverse group of artists from five states, who are also friends of mine and allowed me to introduce their art to a whole new audience.

I thank Black Heritage Gallery and its director Mrs. Stella Miller for giving me another opportunity to curate an exhibition for the gallery and the residents of Lake Charles Louisiana. I hope there will be other exhibitions in the future to share the creative energy of artists from across the country and the globe.

You can view the entire exhibition Online at www.mooboogallery.com

Sálongo Lee
April 7, 2017
www.salongosart.com
www.mooboogallery.com

"Random Samplings: The Group Show 2017"

April 27-May 25, 2017

Opening: Meet The Artists Reception
Friday April 28, 2017

Black Heritage Gallery
The Central School Arts & Humanities Center
809 Kirby Street; Ste. 207
Lake Charles, Louisiana 70601
Monday-Friday: 9:00AM-5:00PM

Mrs. Stella Miller: Director
Sálongo Lee: Guest Curator

Ron Chapman

Chalmette, LA

Frank Jackson

Los Angeles, CA

Randell Henry

Baton Rouge, LA

George Larkins, II

Harlem, NY

Sálongo Lee

Natchez, MS

Gregory Robinson, Jr.

Ferriday, LA

Ron Witherspoon

Atlanta, GA

MonaLisa Whitaker

Inglewood, CA

Katelynn Yvon

Natchez, MS

Ron Chapman:
www.ronchapmanartist.com

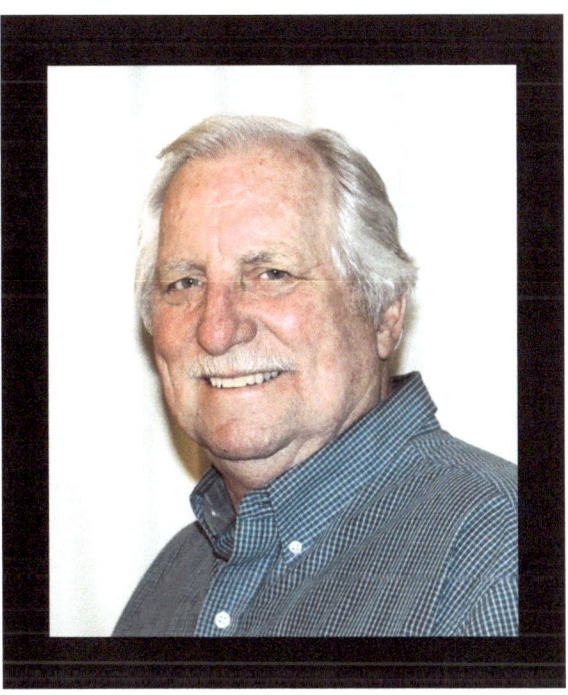

I am Ron Chapman, a Professor of History at Nunez Community College for the past 17 years. I also own a small business for the past 40 years where I manufacture boats. This, in itself, is another expression of art because boats are functional art…a form of sculpture. Additionally, I always held a deep appreciation and interest in the fine arts. I have worked in a variety of mediums including: oils, watercolor, pastels, Chinese Brush painting, pottery, and stained glass throughout my life. My mother was an artist and always encouraged my curiosity.

Sometimes I mix the media in order to derive the result I seek. There are no boundaries in art. Traditional barriers that have existed are meant to be breached in the artist's effort to articulate his inner self.

Artists are a reflection of the society in which they live. Throughout history artists have mirrored the social, political, and technological realities of the world. Our work is an introspective response to stimulus. Sometimes it is emotional, on others intellectual. Artists are a barometer, a means to measure society's tensions, loves, and interests.

I am honored to make my small contribution to this all important element of human society.

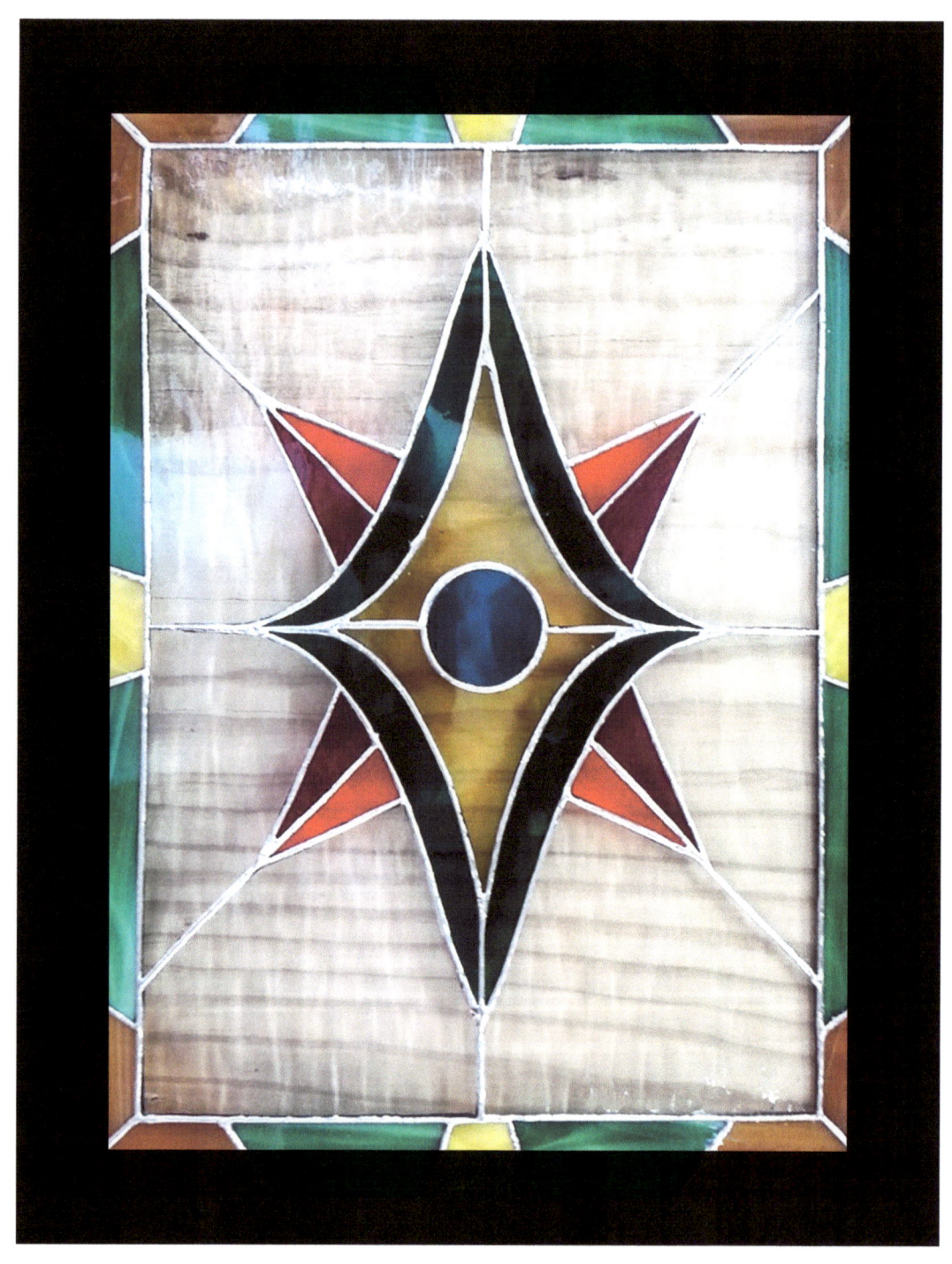

"Stained Glass"   22″x17″   Stained Glass $275.00

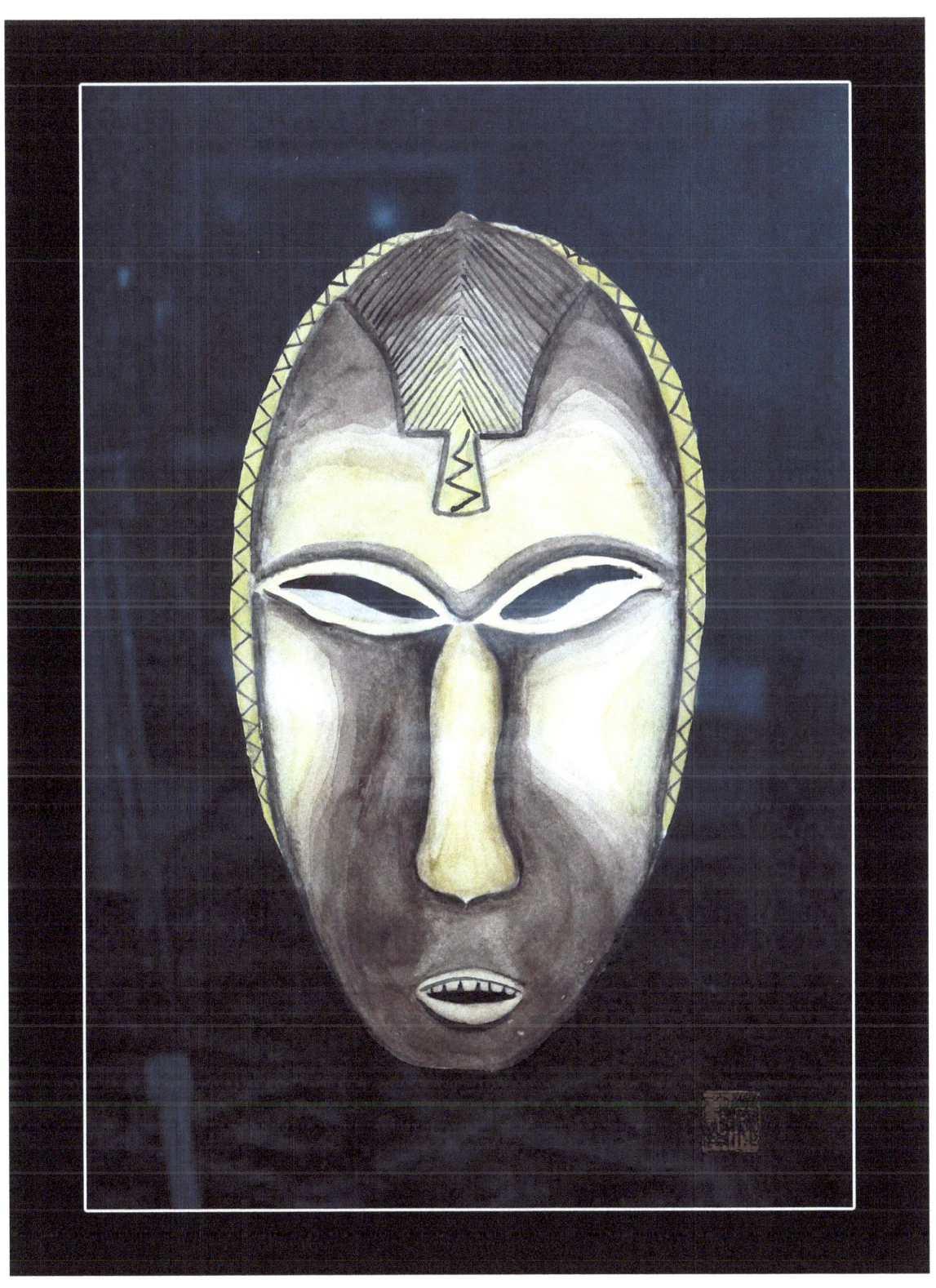

"African Mask"   18″x22″   Watercolor $275.00

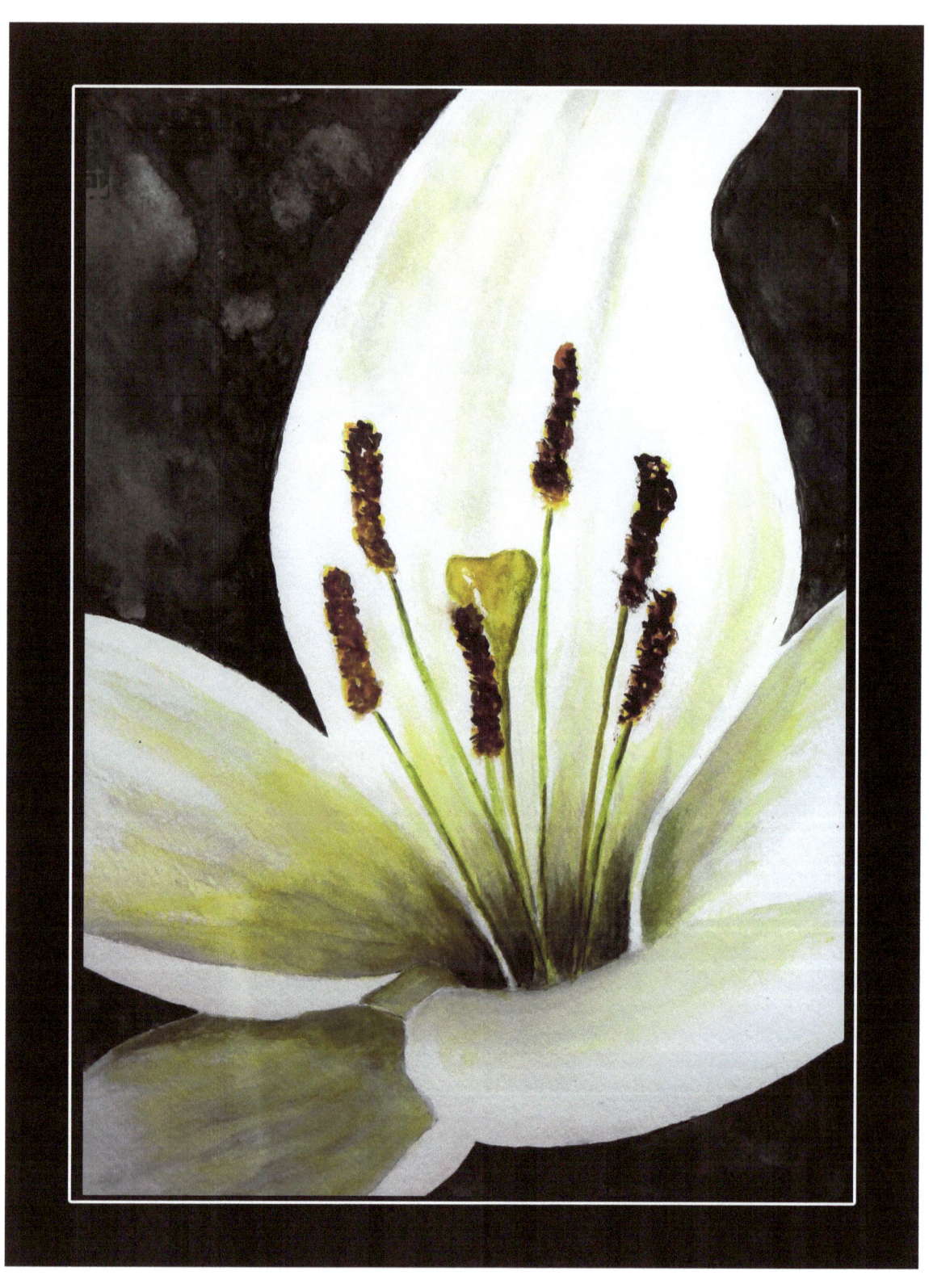

"Flower"   19 1/2"x 23 1/2"   Watercolor $275.00

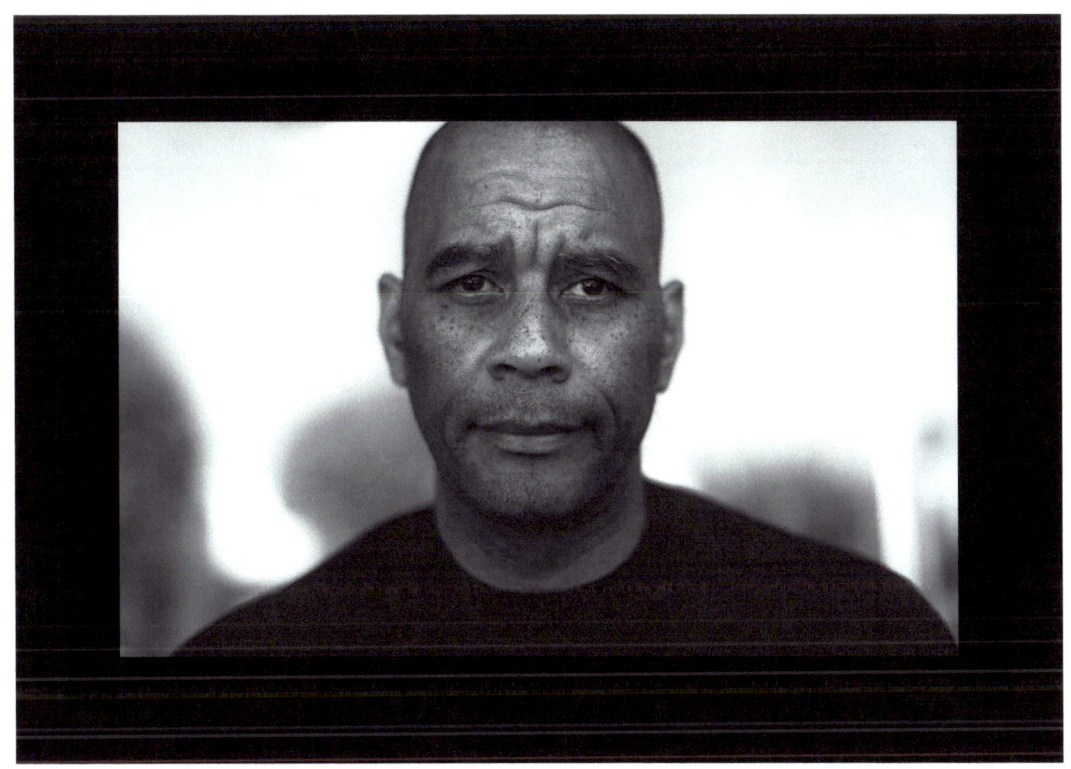

Frank Jackson Ubiquity

www.fotographzfrankjackson.tumbler.com

I can show you more about who I am visually than I could ever tell you. (…or you'd want to listen too….) If there is a word to best define my photography it would be Ubiquitous = present, appearing, or found everywhere. I am constantly seeking a person, place or thing wherever and the subject matters not because its all about the light. There are three main types of light: sunlight, man made, and not much. I have learned to appreciate and work with all three because only light really defines what can make a photograph special.

Photography is the active capture of a single moment…and I am simply happy to become the sum of my moments.

Frank Jackson

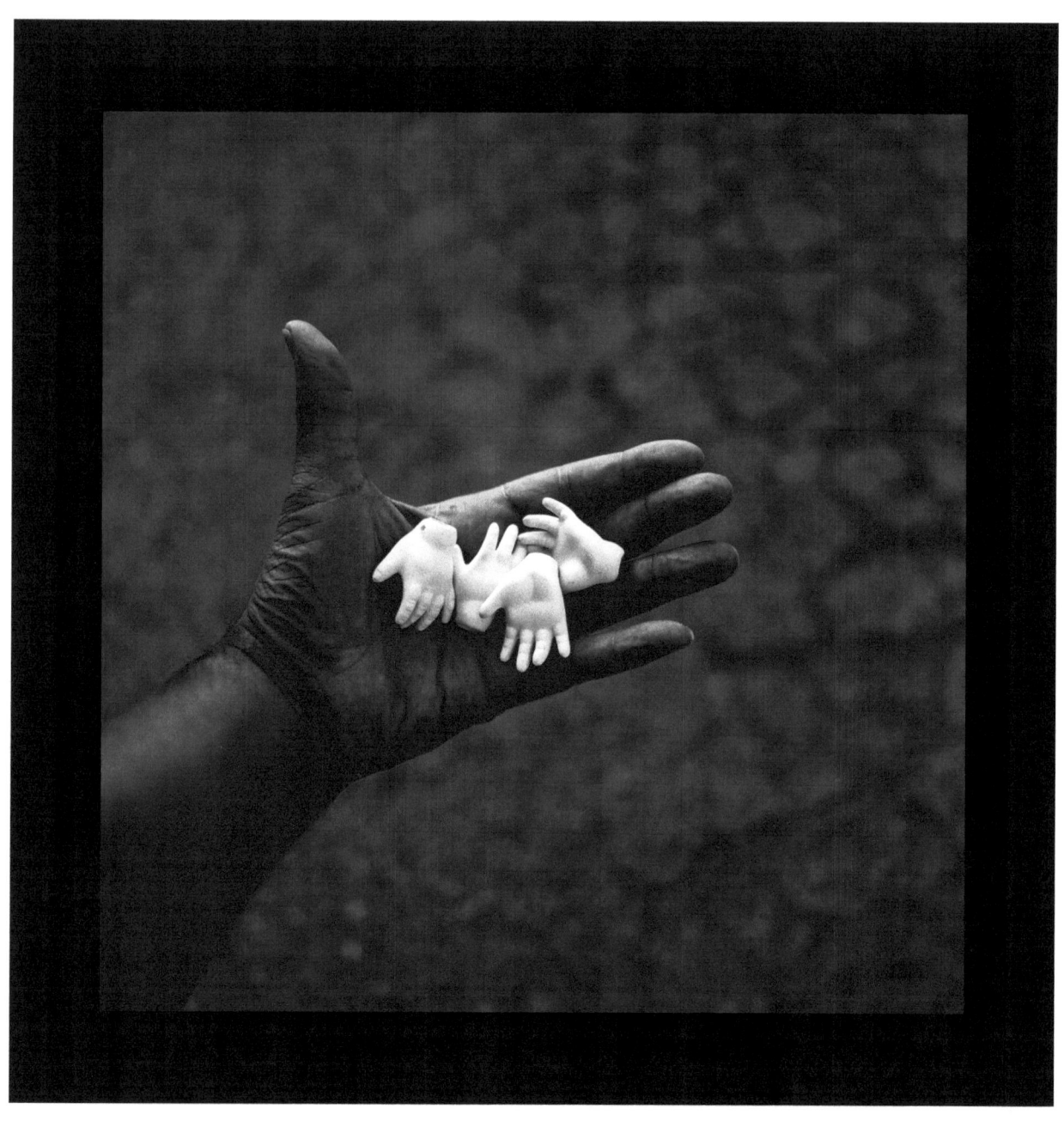

"Hand To Mouth"   Image Size 8.75″x8.75″ B&W Photograph in 16″x20″
In White Matt LE of 10 $250.00

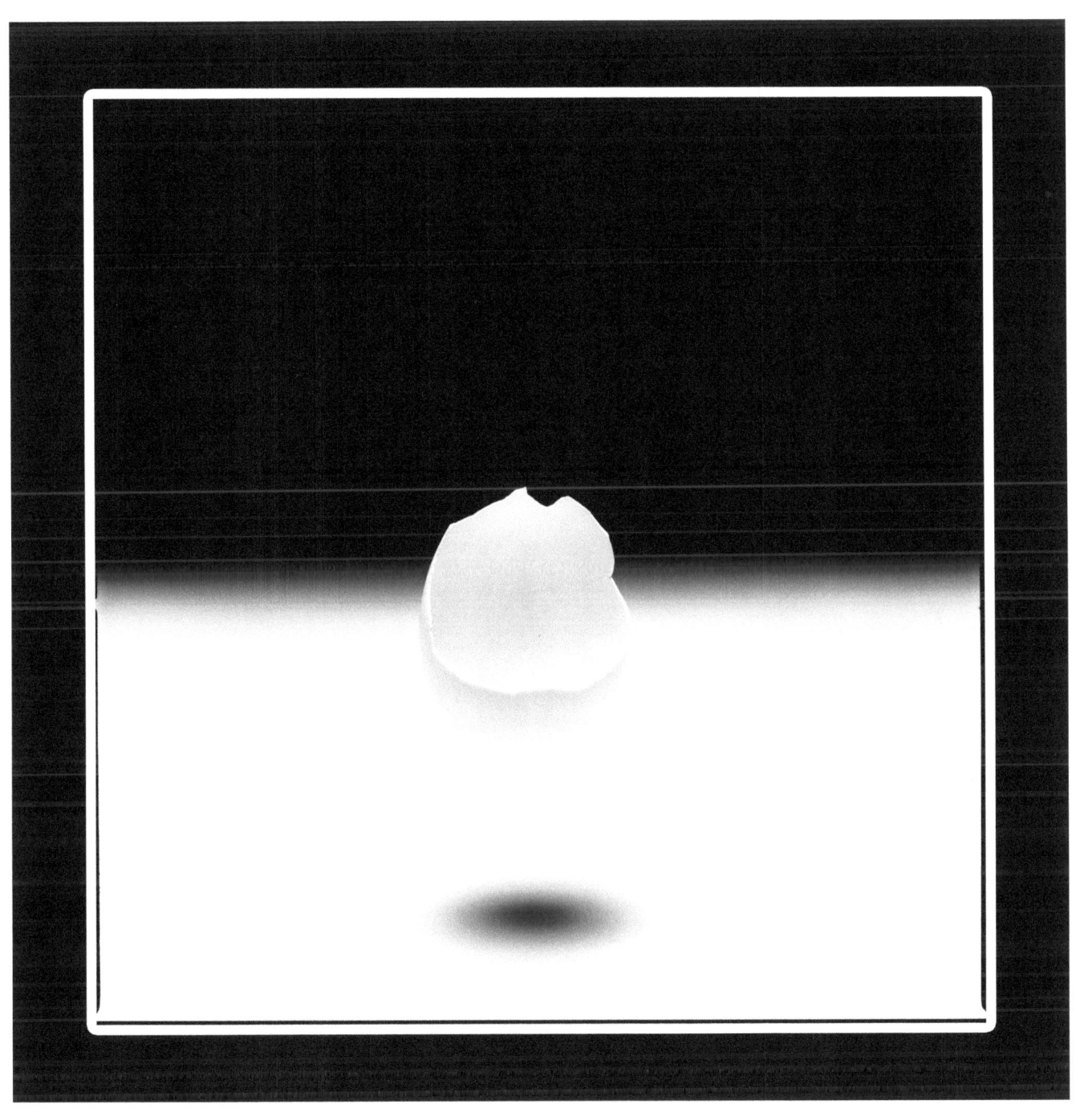

"Balance"   Image Size 8.75″x8.75″ B&W Photograph
In White 16″x20″ Matt LE of 10 $250.00

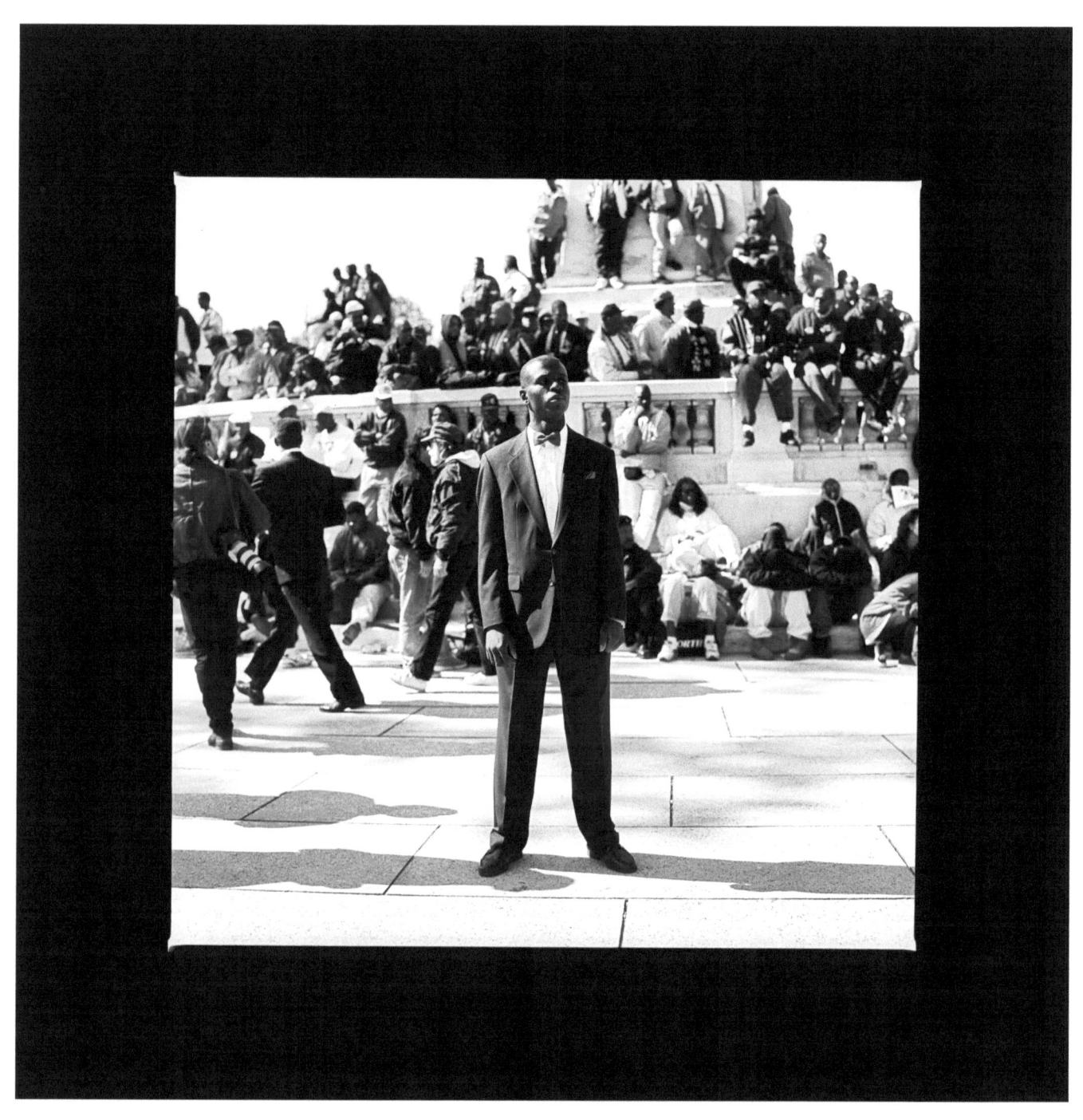

"One Man, Million Man March   1996"   Image Size 8.75″x8.75″ B&W Photograph
In White 16″x20″ Matt LE of 10 $250.00

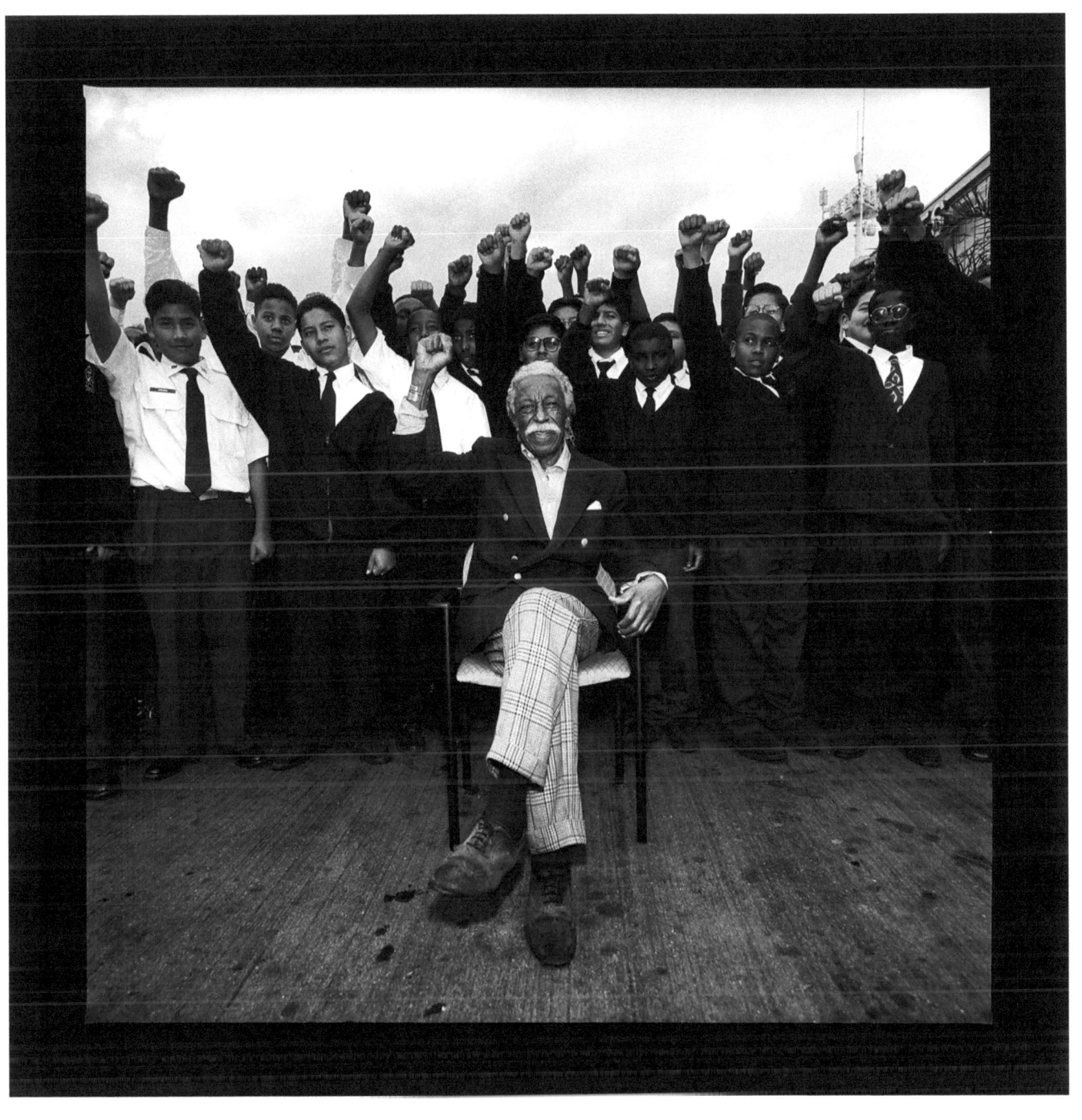

"Gordon Parks"   Image Size 8.75″x8.75″ B&W Photograph
In White Matt 16″x20″ Matt LE of 10 $250.00

Randell Henry

www.batonrougegallery.org

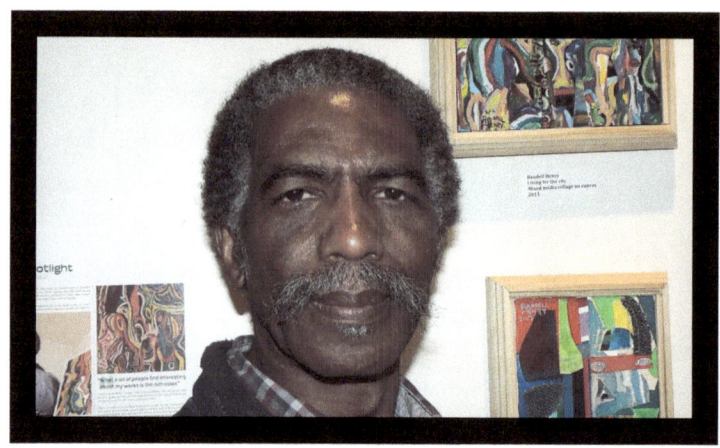

Randell Henry set his dreams on a career in the visual arts and decided to become a painter when he was a sixth grade kid in 1969. In junior high and high school he headed straight to the library every chance he got, pulling art books off the shelves to study the paintings of Jackson Pollock, Franz Kline, Robert Motherwell, Hans Hofmann, Marc Chagall, Pablo Picasso, and many American painters who used abstraction in their work. Henry earned a B.A. in Fine Arts from Southern University and a MFA in Painting and Drawing from Louisiana State University.

Henry is Associate Professor of Visual Arts and Curator of the Southern University Visual Arts Gallery at Southern. He has curated many exhibitions of art by local, national and international artists, including by Romare Bearden, Jacob Lawrence, Lois Mailou Jones, John Biggers, Elizabeth Catlett, William Tolliver, Henry O. Tanner, Richard Mayhew, James Denmark. Henry had his first major one man exhibition in May, 1982 after walking into Nahan Galleries in New Orleans and showing one of his collages to owner, Kenneth Nahan. This was the first time that this exclusive French Quarter gallery had ever featured an unknown artist in an exhibition. Ironically, the exhibition followed a major Picasso show.

In 1991, fifteen of his paintings where featured in an exhibition at the New Orleans Museum of Art. A few years later Henry Dr. Stella Jones, featured hiswork in her St. Charles Street Gallery. Over the years Jones hasfeatured his paintings and collages both, in gallery exhibitions and at art fairs and special exhibitions around the U.S. A large painting by Henry, along with works by other artists from Stella Jones Gallery were included in exhibitions at Macy's Department Stores in New Orleans and Houston in Spring 2012, along with works by Romare Bearden to celebrate the one hundredth anniversary of the birth of Bearden.

In 2014,his work was included in Visual Blues, an exhibition of works by famous African American artists of the Harlem Renaissance. In 2015 three of his works were included in an exhibition at The Louisiana Arts and Science Museum to highlight contemporary abstract artists from Baton Rouge who have made an impact on the vibrant Louisiana art scene. In May 2016, Henry work's was featured in "60 Americans," a national exhibition of recognized artists heldin New Yourk City. New York Times Art Critic Roberta Smith as Henry's work as her favorite work in the show.

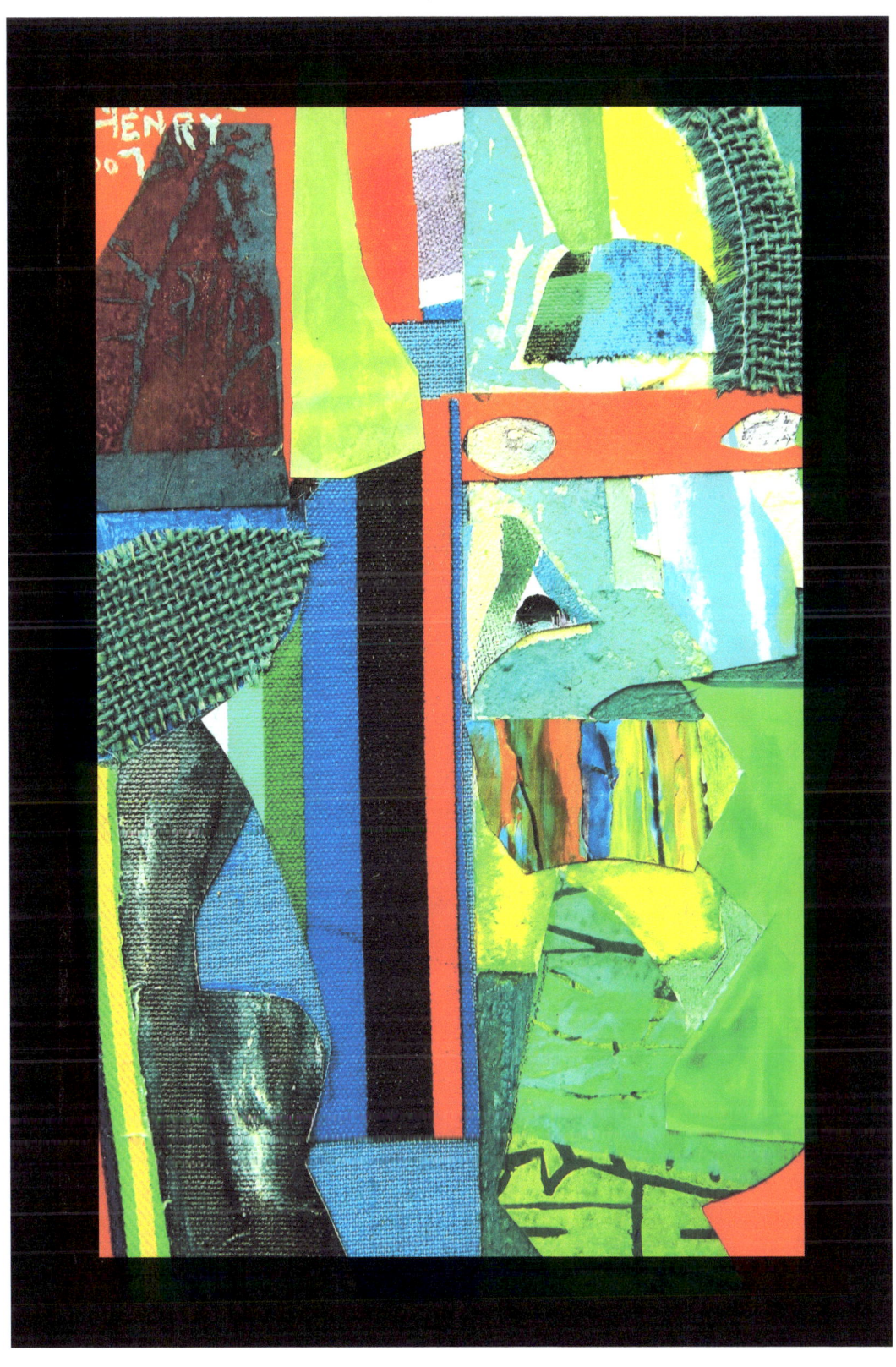

"Warrior"   2007   Mixed Media Collage on Canvas   9"H x 6"W $900

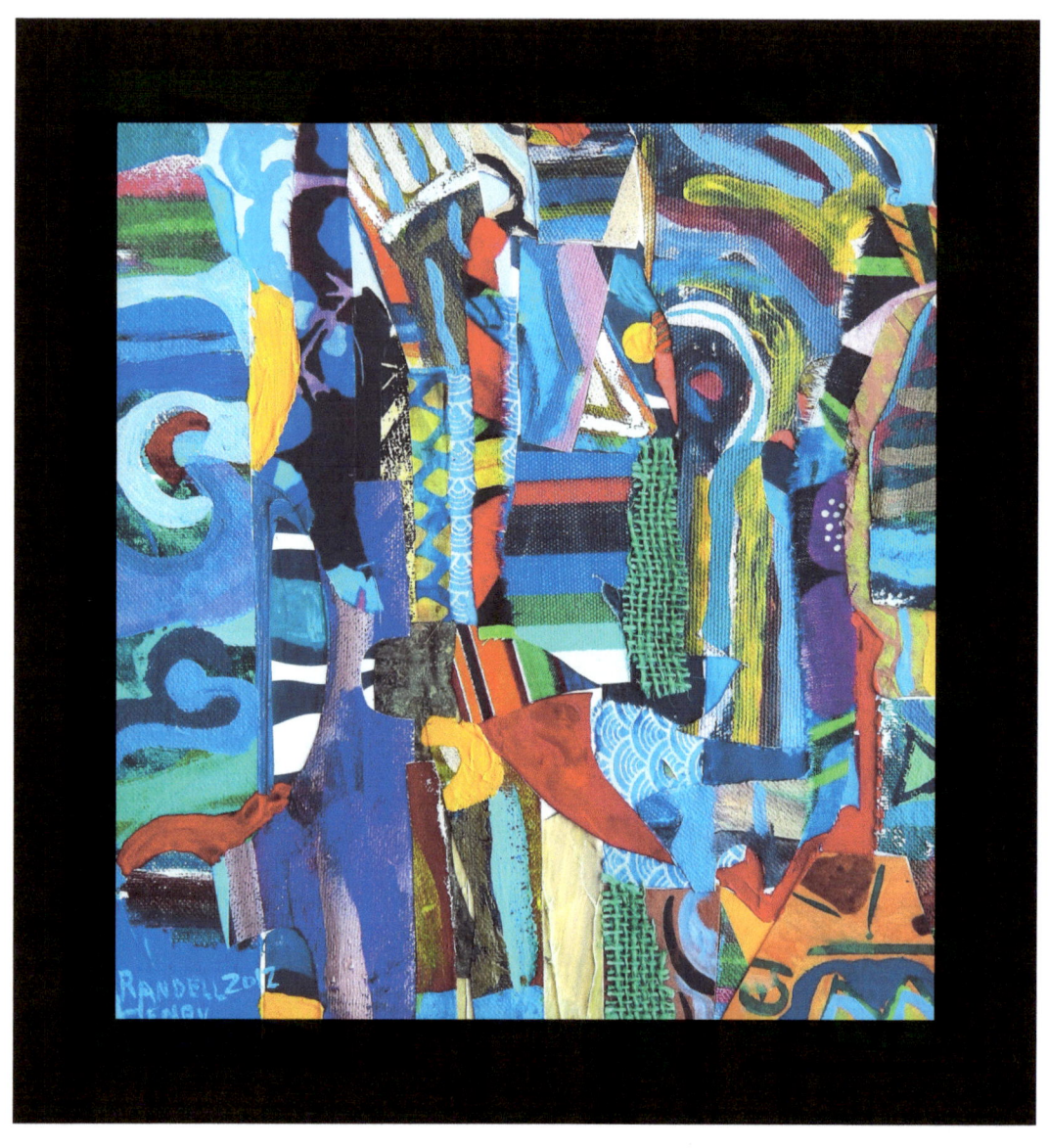

"Night Dreams"   2012   Mixed Media Collage on Canvas   9"H x 9"W $1250

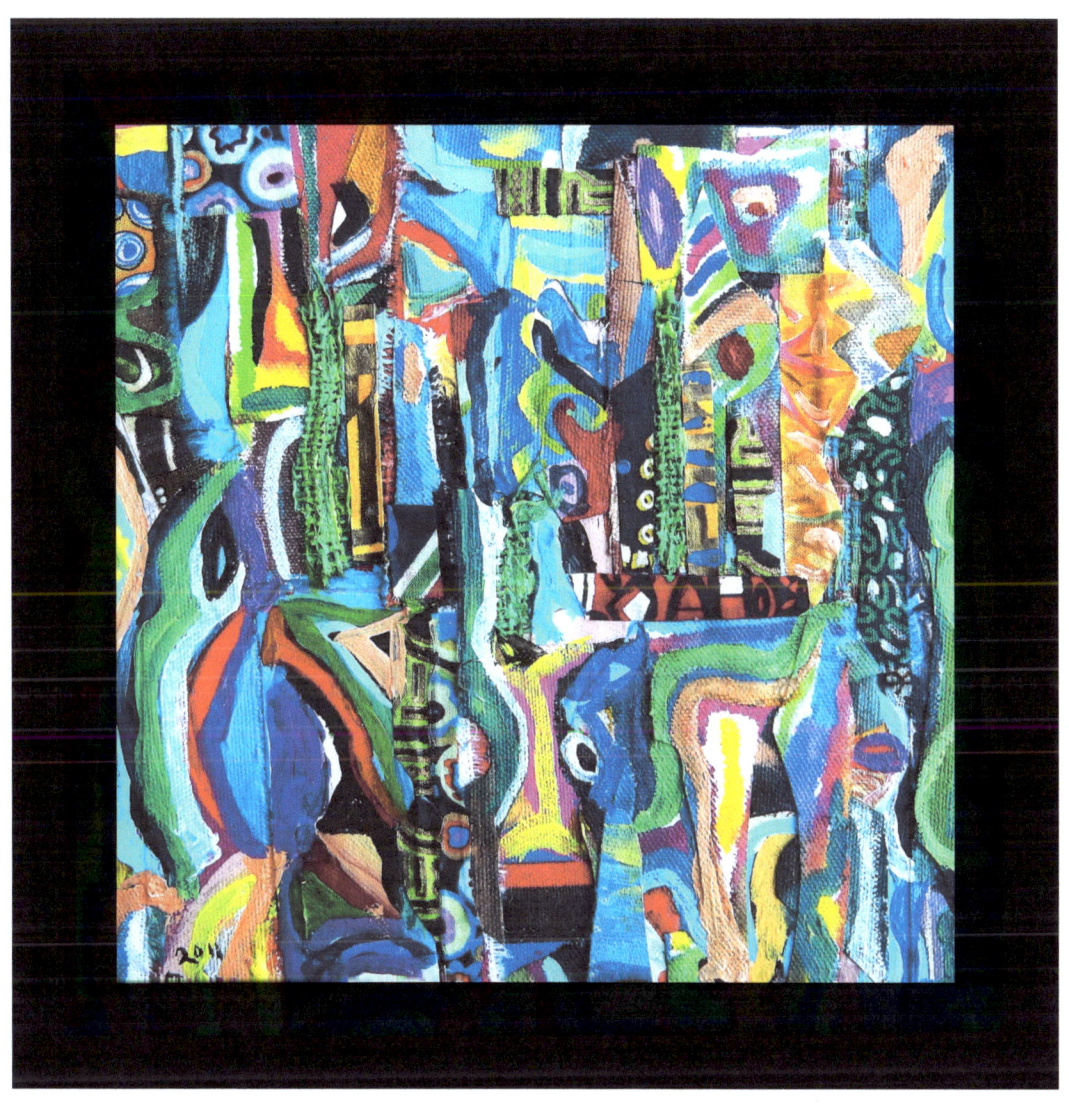

"Living For The City"   2012   Mixed Media Collage on Canvas   9″H x 9″W $1250

George Larkins, II

My arts education began in my own independent study of photography and the world of image production as a photo assistant. I was drawn to the storytelling properties of images and in the way that an image could challenge a viewer's thinking, sense of self, and understanding of the world. I then was fortunate enough to attend the Art Center College of Design in Pasadena, California, where I earned my B.F.A. in Photography. This program introduced me to the primacy of concept development, the power of research, and the discipline of honing technical competence to carry out my vision in my work. Later, during my M.F.A. program at Pratt Institute in Brooklyn, I began to expand from the analog into the digital world of image making, first through an investigation of digital photography, then through experimentation with Photoshop and motion graphics software for time-based digital image making. My thesis show combined large-format photography and prints with

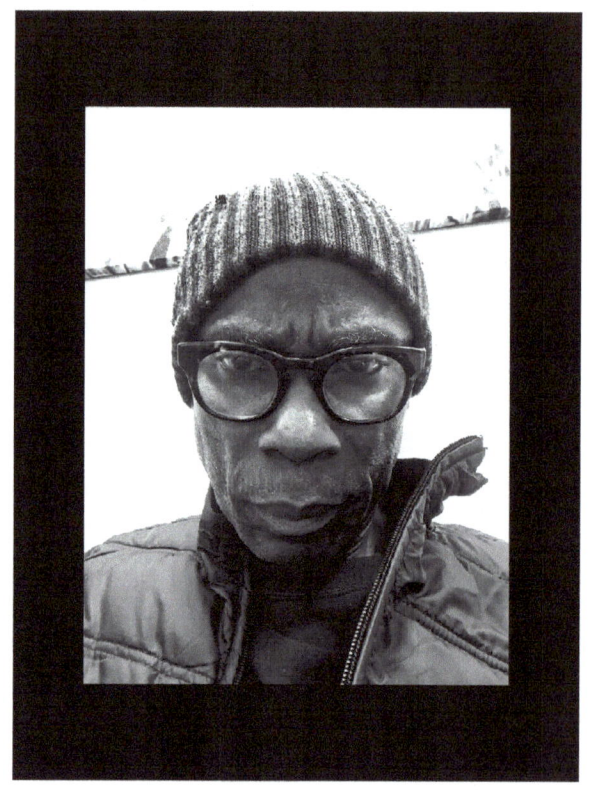

a digital video piece that depicted time, beauty and decay. The digital video portrayed individual journeys through an urban setting, and introduced images of insects and type elements to represent archival records of time.

My passion for what I do has enabled me to create digital and analog art over the years through my travels abroad and I while spending summers working in Paris. Indeed an enriching experience. Along with photography I have created digital visual components for live dance and music performance pieces. I have created short films that weave together film imagery and digital components, such as type and geometric and organic shapes. I have infused my commercial work with my interest in the tension between the appealing and disturbing, and I continue to find the combination of the analog and the digital endlessly inspiring. I was a selected participant in the School of Visual Arts Residency Program in Sculpture and New Media where I created dystopian 3D images dealing with insanity. From that I was chosen as a highlighted artist by a Venezuelan television feature of the program's exhibition as well as in SVA's own media blasts. I am also a tenure track professor at New York City Tech.

www.grlstudio.com   &   www.behance.net/grlstudio

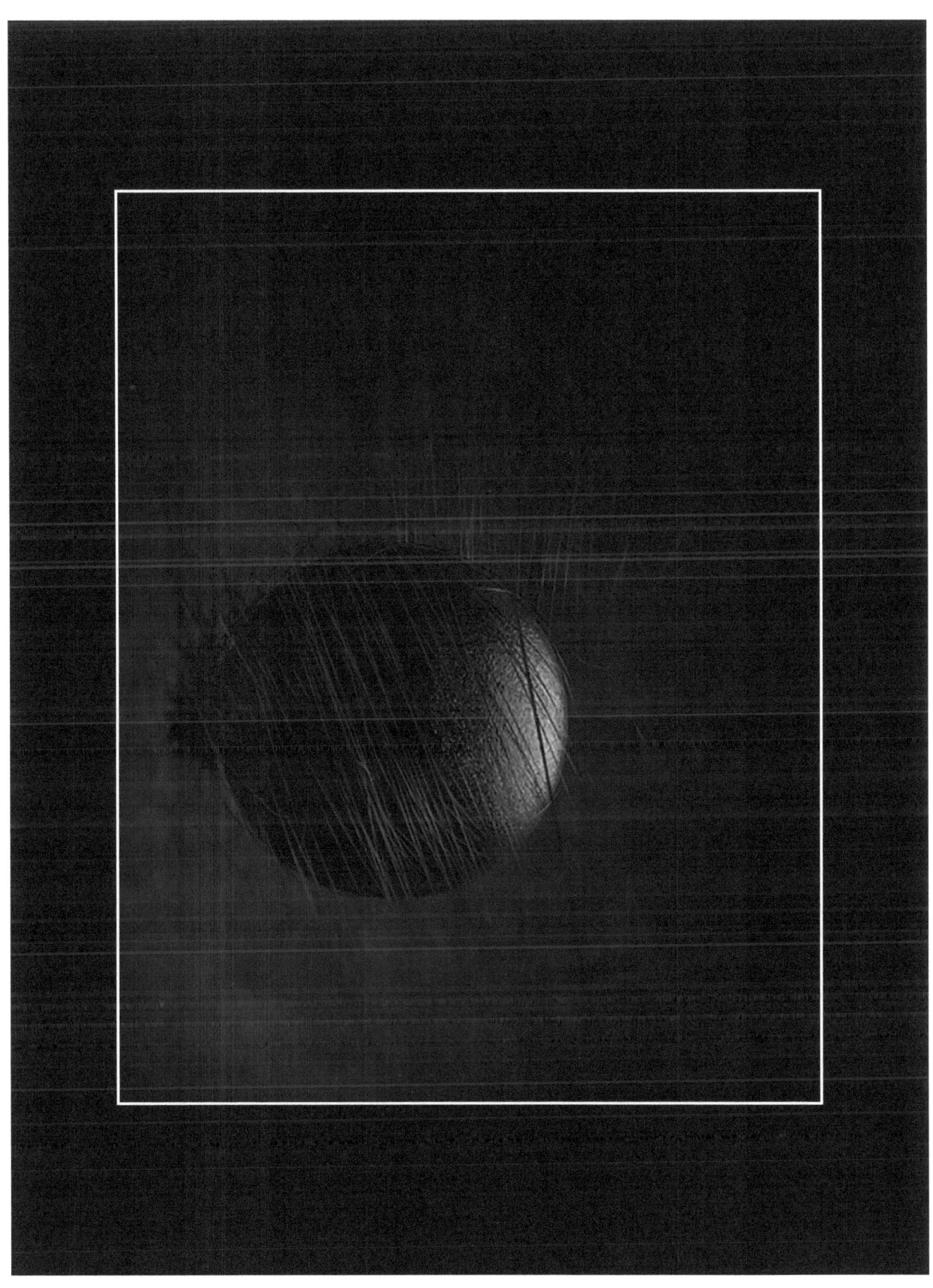

"My Sanity"   16″x20″   B&W Photograph $400.00

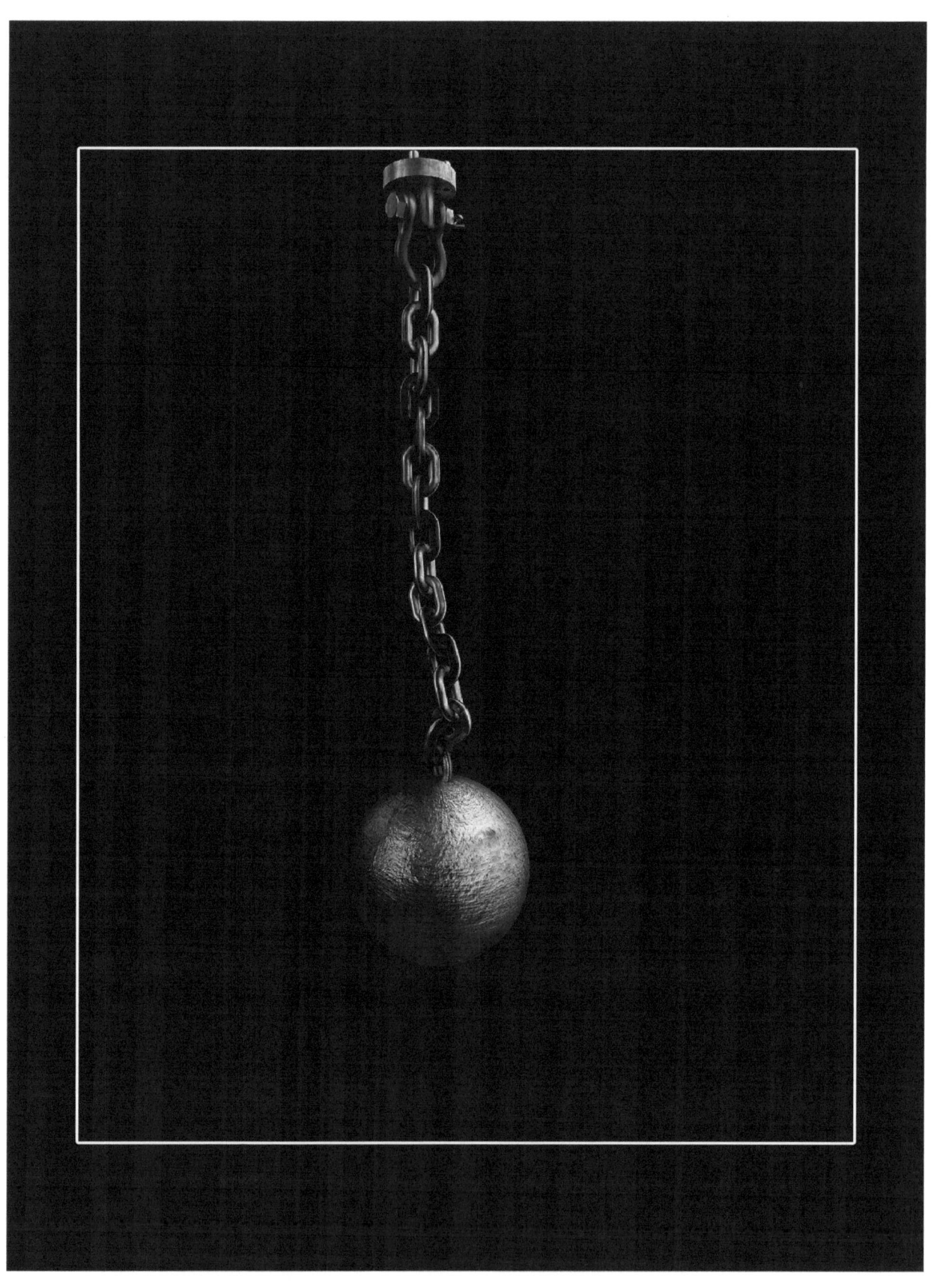

"Ball & Chain Nightmare"   16″x20″ B&W Photograph $400.00

(18)

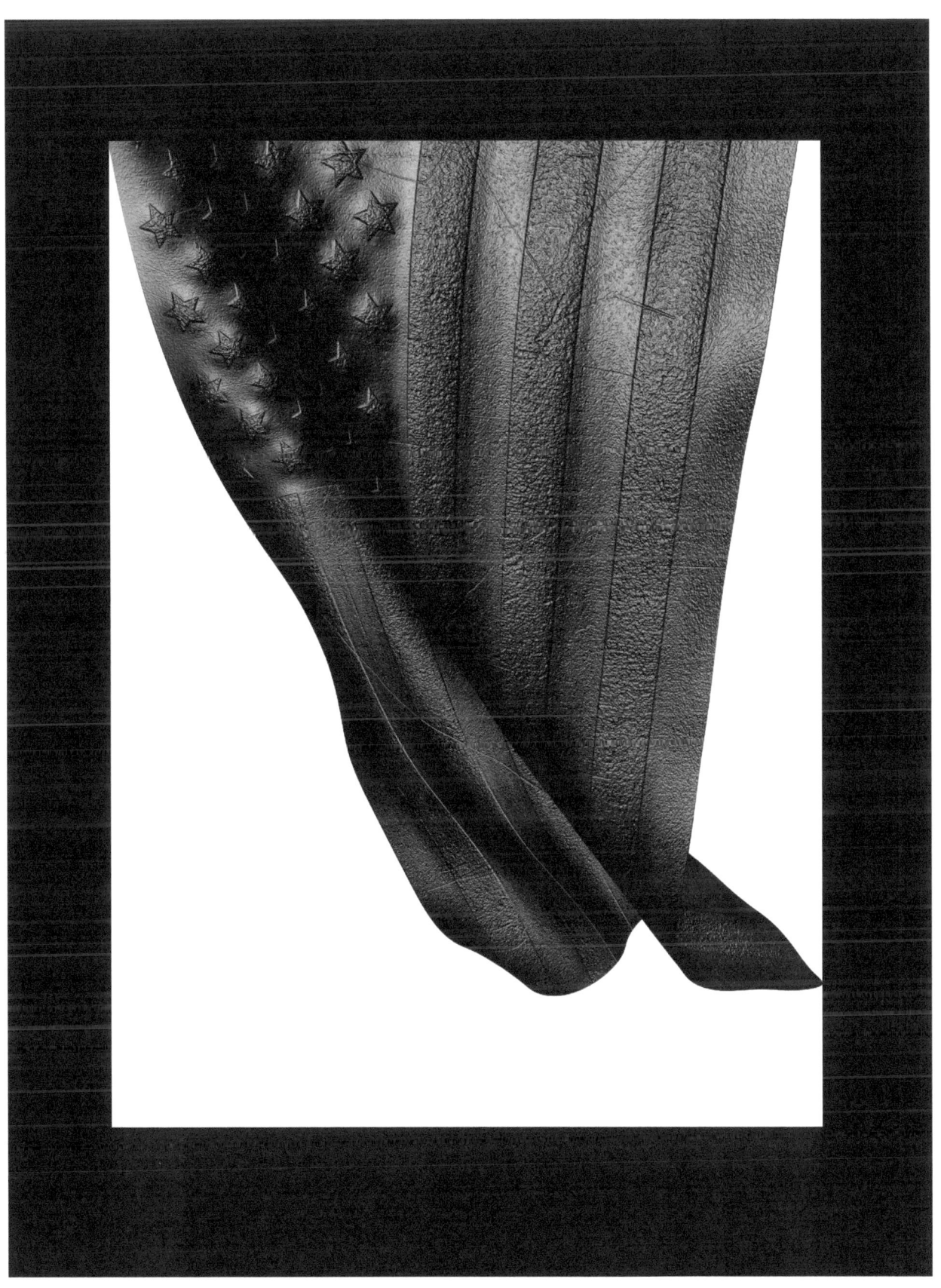

"Flag of My Ancestors"   16″x20″ B&W Photograph $400.00

(19)

Sálongo Lee
Guest Curator

www.salongosart.com
www.salongoleephotography.com

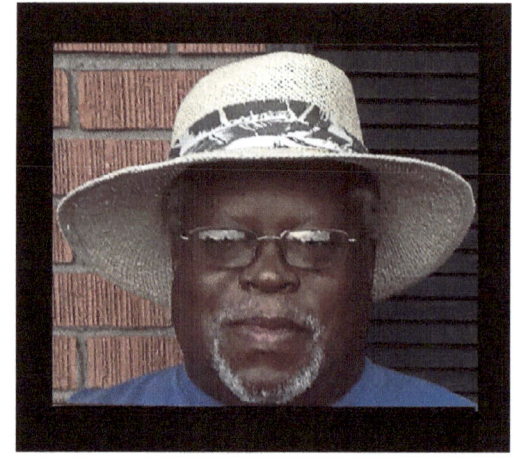

Photography has been a part of my life for over forty-five years, it's my mistress, my other love and my spiritual companion. It is an affair that has no end, which allows me to speak to the world in ways that can touch the soul without the need of spoken words. It gives voice to the visions of my Third Eye. I can reach out from my subconscious and show the world things that may change lives in little ways

My career as a commercial photographer, photojournalist, performance photograher shooting dance and theater production spanned twenty-five years. I covered Nelson Mandela's and Pope John Paul ll's visit to Los Angeles as well as the 1989 San Francisco/ Oakland earthquake. I was in Oakland for the funeral of Dr. Huey P. Newton (co-founder of the Black Panther Party) and the gang violence on the streets of South Central Los Angeles. I toured as company photographer for a regional dance company and covered the Hollywood Entertainment scene as a staff writer/photographer. I've taught photography and arts & crafts to adults and children for a number of arts organizations. I have owned a gallery, managed several other galleries and seen my work published in books and magazines.

My true love has been creating images, telling stories with images and finding ways to bring what I see in my subconscious, with my Third Eye into existence in the real world. In the mid 1990's, I attended CSU San Francisco as an art major, studying photography as a fine arts medium and taking classes in printmaking and sculpture. Now photography is just one of my creative tools. I use multiple creative mediums such as sculpture, my original Haiku Poetry, mixed media constructions and photography to touch people souls. Now I see myself as a visual artist, something I never saw myself becoming. I also have come to enjoy creating opportunities for other emerging and mid career artists to share their creativity with new audiences across the country.

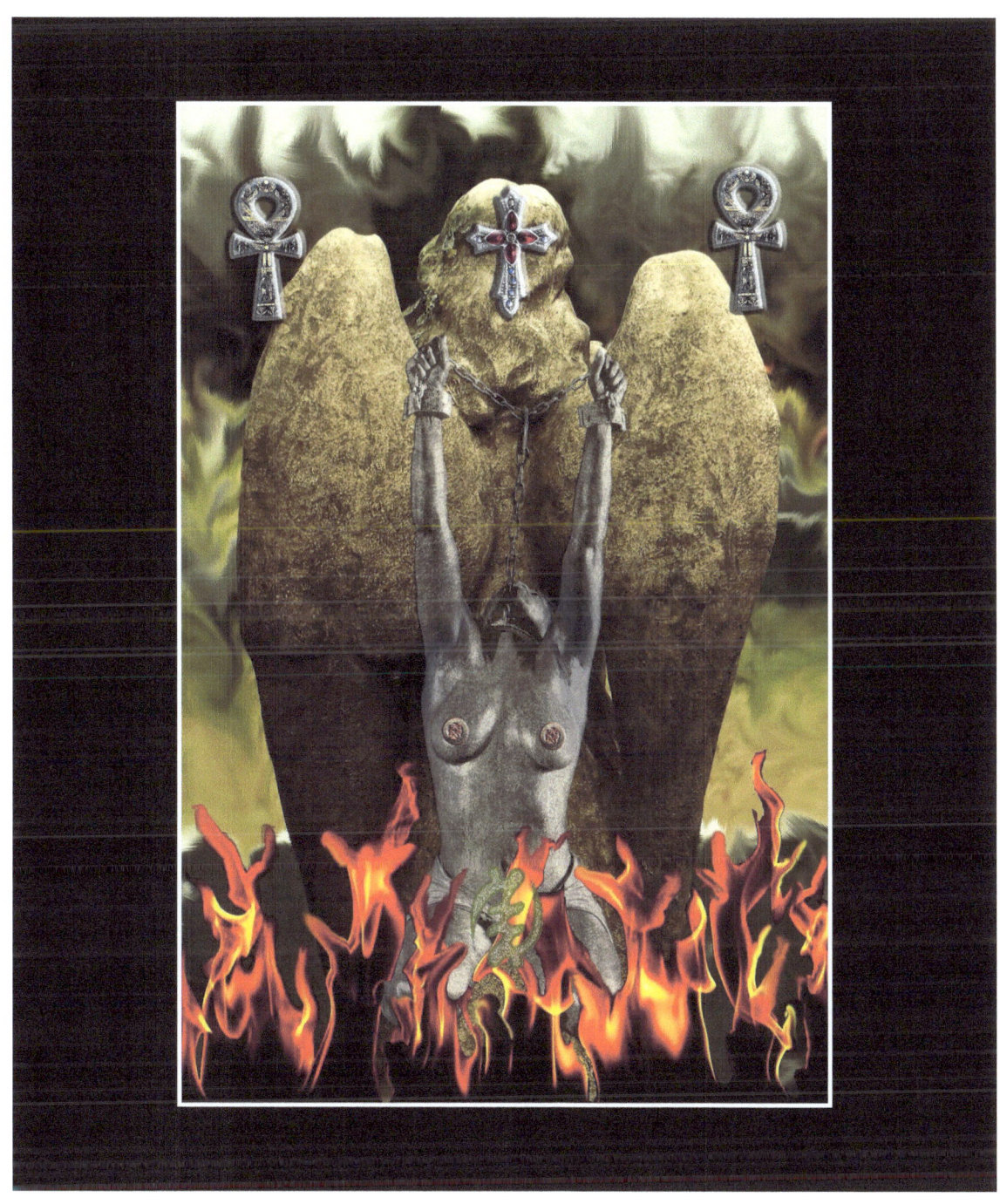

"Shelter Me Under Your Wings, Oh Lord"   16″x24″ LE/10 S&N
Photograph On Canvas $500.00

Inspired by Tab Benoit's "Shelter Me" from his album "power of the pontchartrain". The Image of the slave woman was created in 1990 and the statue of the angel was taken in 2007 in the Natchez City Cemetery in Natchez, MS. This image represents the Slaves enduring the hell of slavery, while praying for salvation, that usually came only at death. The Adinkra symbols, wh were the slaves one connection to their culture that could not be taken from them.

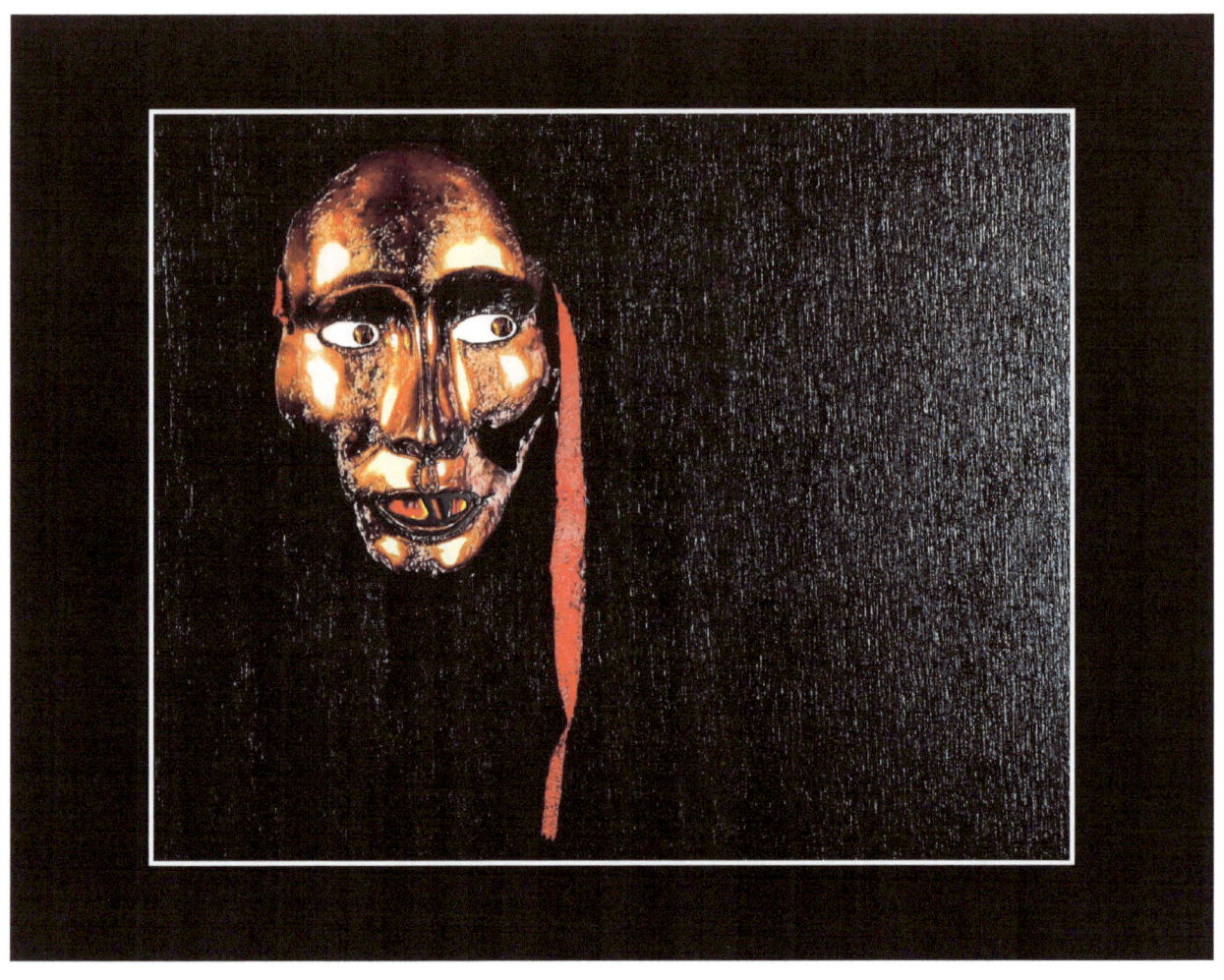

"I See You"   16″x20″   Photograph on Canvas LE/10 S&N $500.00

This is Mask #92 from my 100 Mask Series, which began in 2009. The series is a countdown to Mask #1, that began with Masks #100, #99 & #98. I am inspired by images of masks and objects that could be worn as a mask; even things that occur in nature. I plan to devote the next year to the project. When it is completed I will have an exhibition and publish a book of the images.

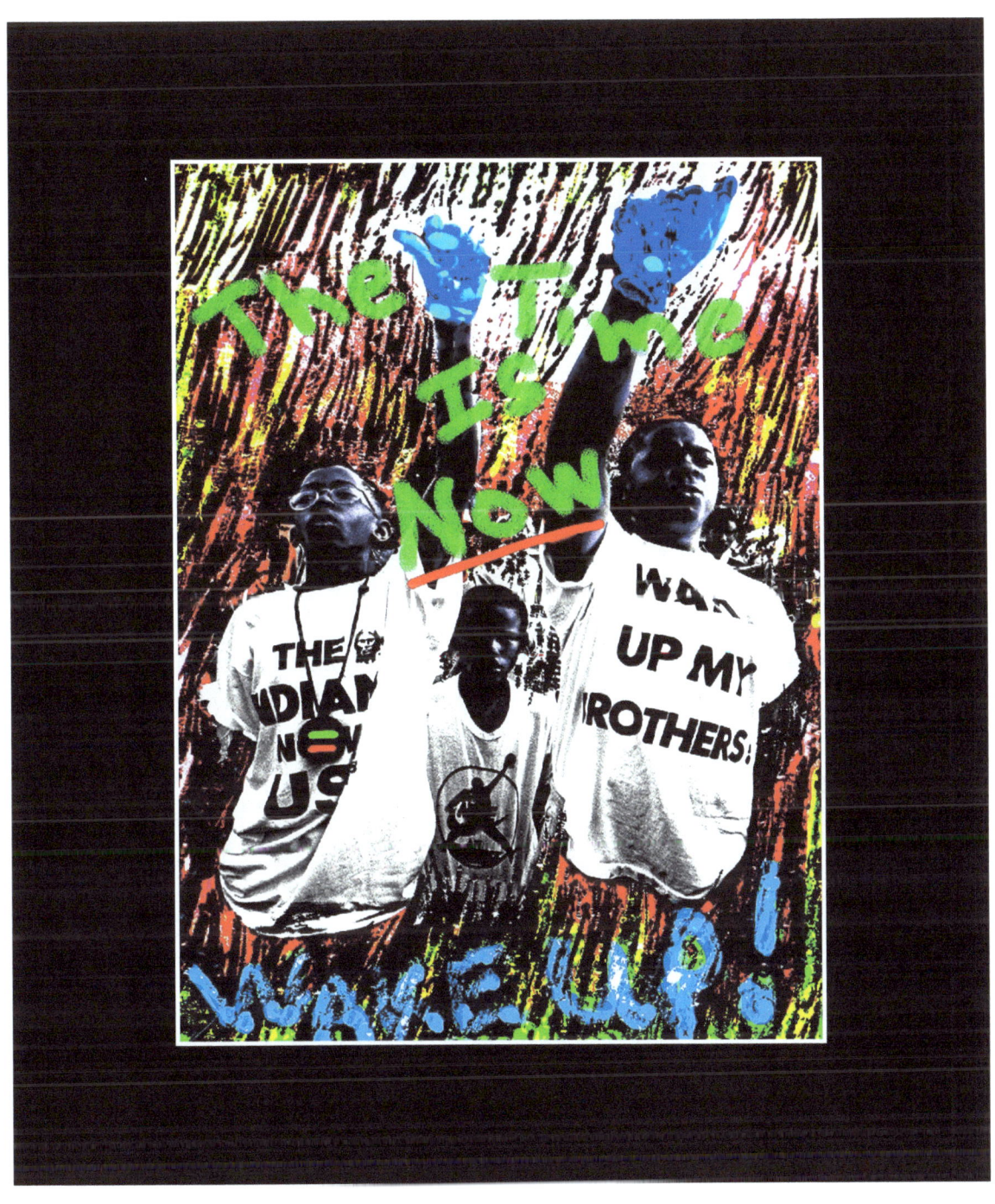

"Wake Up, Now!"   12″x16″   Color Photograph on Canvas Printed From
A Hand Painted B&W 35mm Film Negative LE/75 S&N $100.00
It is time for all of us to wake up and take charge of our lives, our families and
to take charge of our country!.

Gregory Robinson, Jr.
www.facebook.com/Greg-Robinson-Jr-

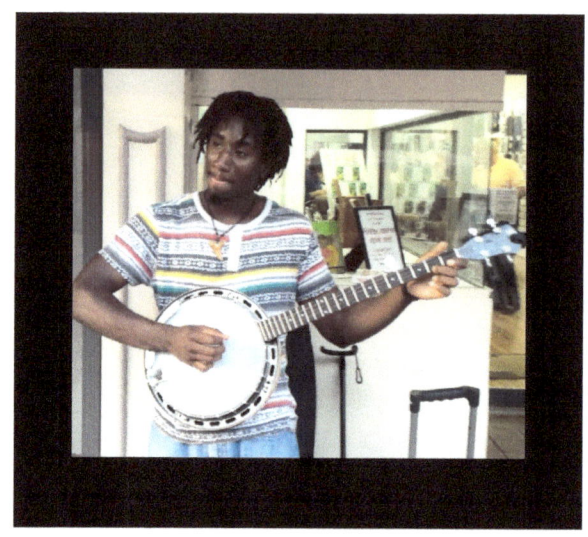

Greg Robinson, Jr. is a visual artist/musician born in Metairie, Louisiana and raised in Ferriday, Louisiana. His style of art is what you will call primitive (cave wall art) also specializing in swamp scenes showcasing vibrant colors to get his point across. Also he makes use of the ancient art of woodburning a technique which at one time was used by people of the Nile Valley or Ancient Egypt. Gregory can be found performing with variuos local bands.

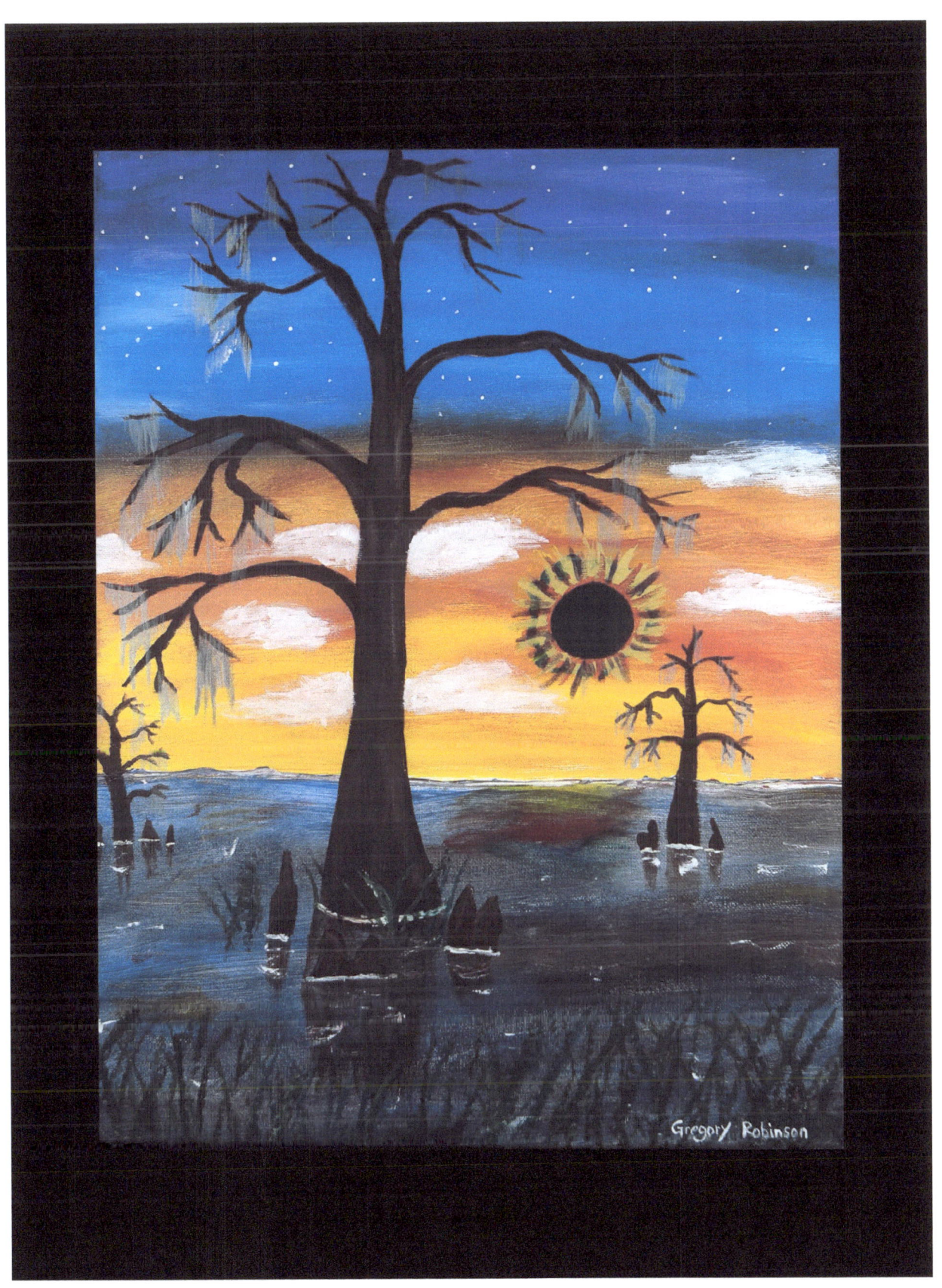

"Serene Swamp"   14″x17 1/2″   Acrylic on Canvas $150.00

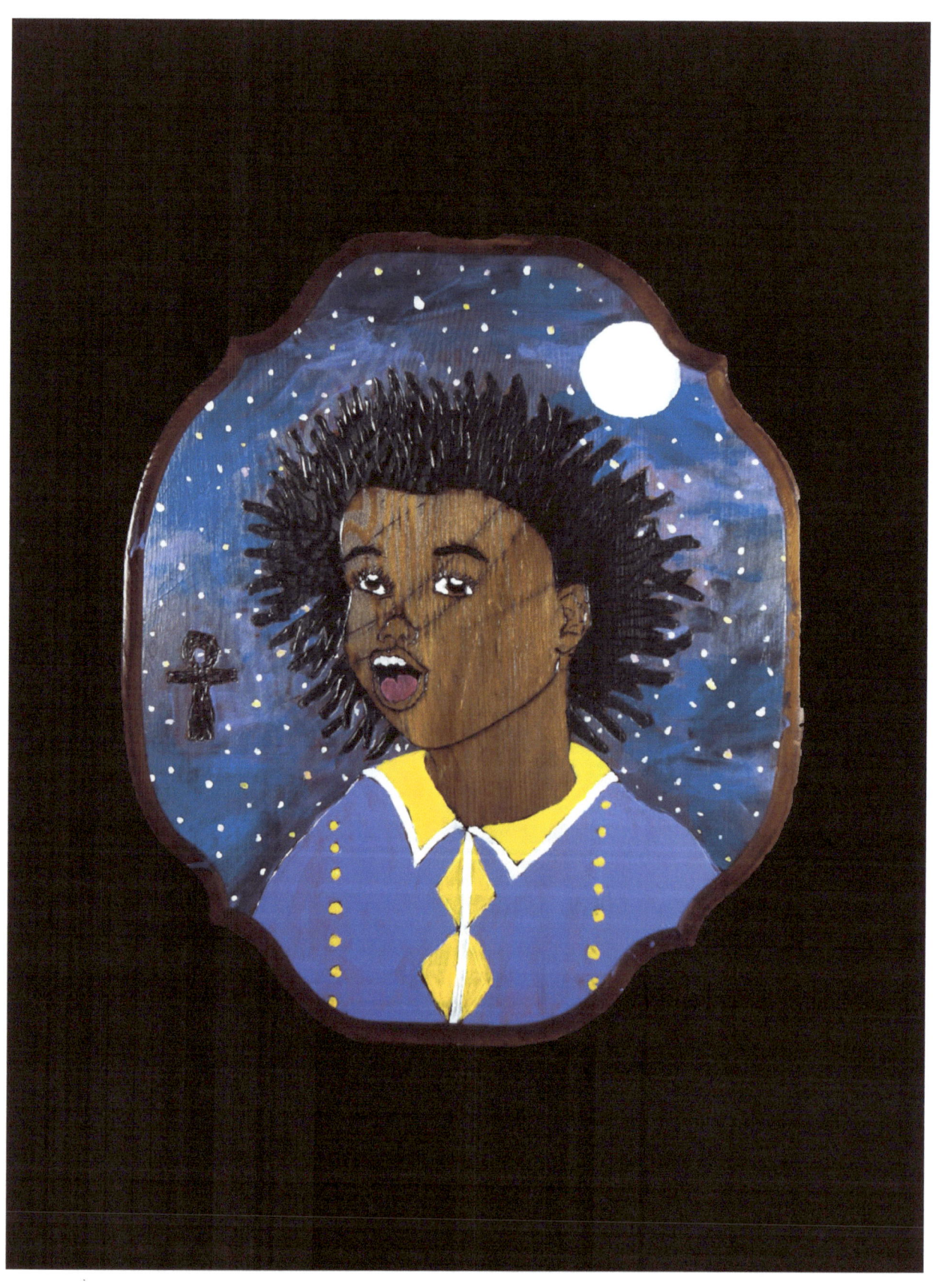

"Gleaming Star of Scars"   11"x13" Wood Burning on Panel $150.00

(26)

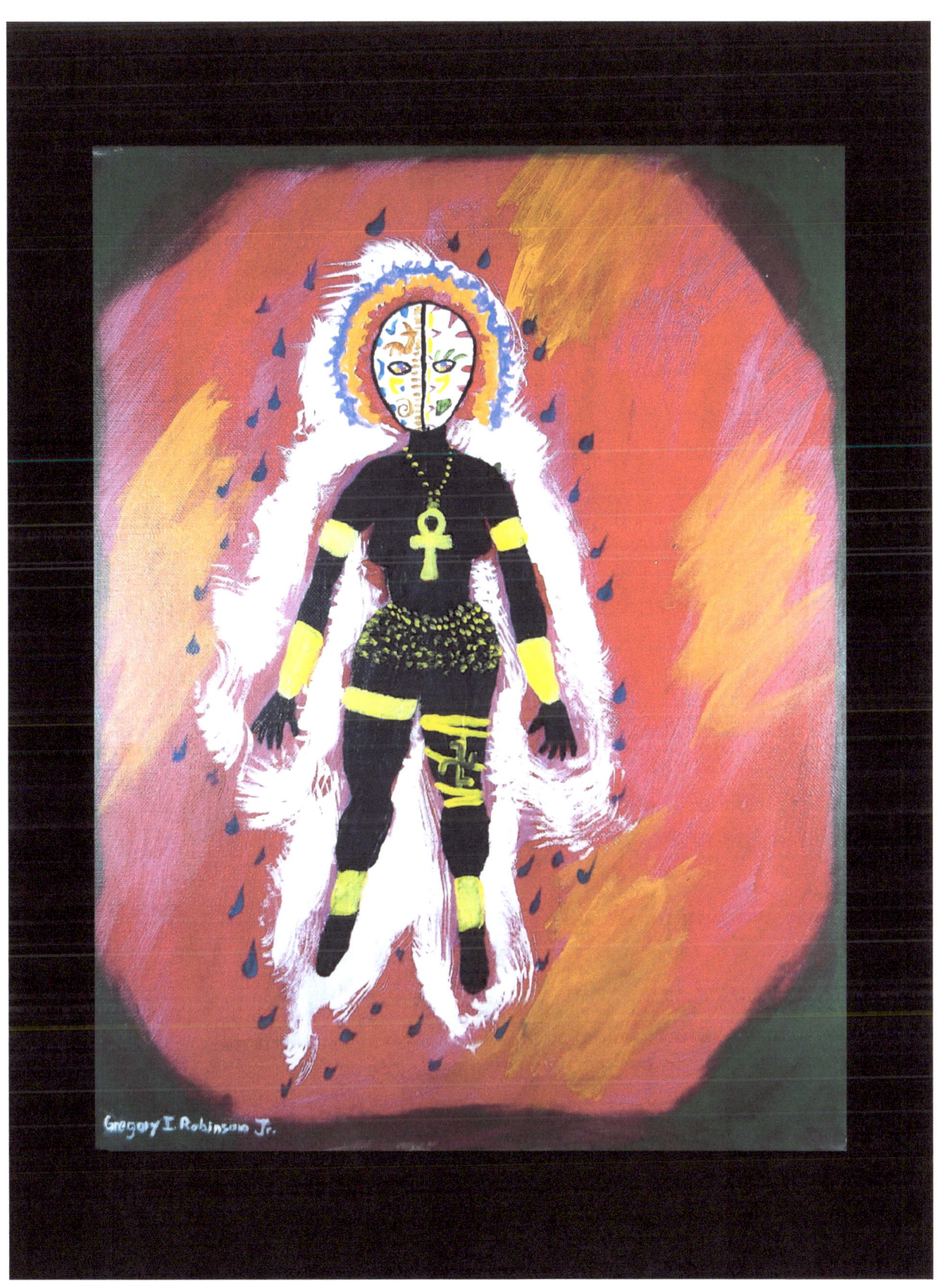

"Empress of Life"   14″x17 1/2″ Acrylic on $150.00

(27)

MonaLisa Whitaker
www.monalisawhitaker.com

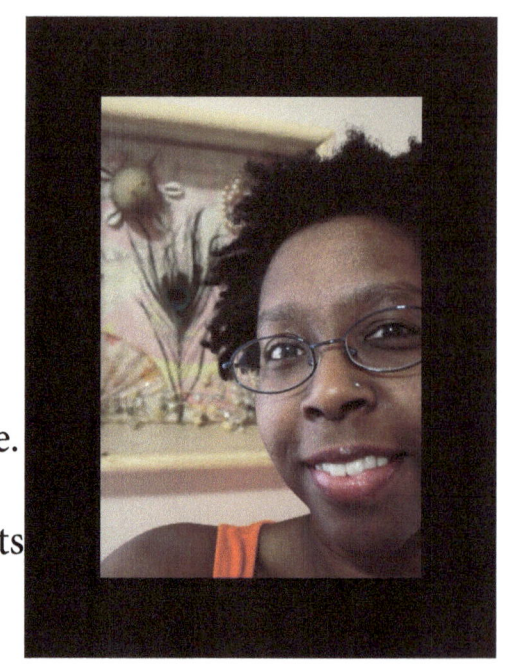

Los Angeles based visual artist working in pho tography and mixed media. Whitaker has a BA in Art History from California State University Dominguez Hills, an AA in Studio Art from El Camino College and an Occupational Certificate in Photography from Santa Monica College. In addition to her creative work, she's an art administrator working with Inglewood Cultural Arts and Watts Labor Community Action Committee and volunteers with a number of community organizations.

She is a dedicated advocate for artists and communities (in the various definitions of diversity-ethnicity, gender, language, country of origin, ability, identity, economic background) and enjoys creating art projects in response to community requests.

Artist Statement:

Visual art is one of the most effective ways to communicate and my preferred mode
of expression. My work usually addresses issues such as questions of identity, sexuality and religion utilizing alternative processes. Thru the use of photographic techniques (hand crafted image and emulsion transfers, sepia toning, printing onto materials other than paper) and digital imaging, I've found that the audience can be inspired or have their perceptions shifted. For the past five years, my work has focused on the individual search for spiritual enlightenment, places of worship and themes of sensuality. My artistic goals are to stimulate the viewers imagination, raise awareness, encourage inquiry and provoke dialogue to promote understanding and acknowledgement that we are all interconnected, despite societal tendencies to perpetuate/focus on our differences.

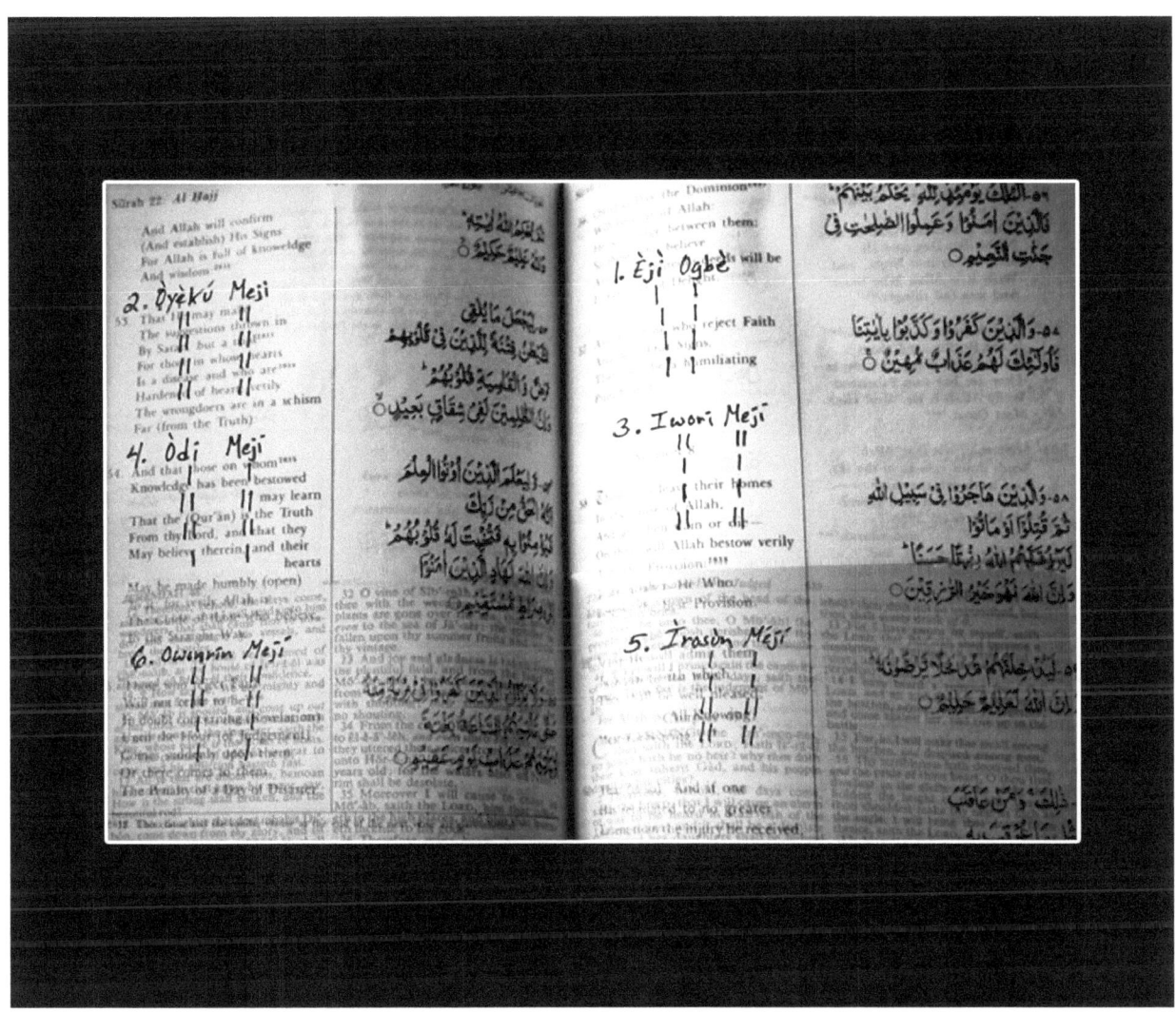

"Sacred Text"   Image Size 8″x10″ on 16″x20″ Media
Multilayered photograph Combining the three religions of Ifa, Islam and Christiani-
ty. Hand printed black & white photograph, with permanent marker. $450.

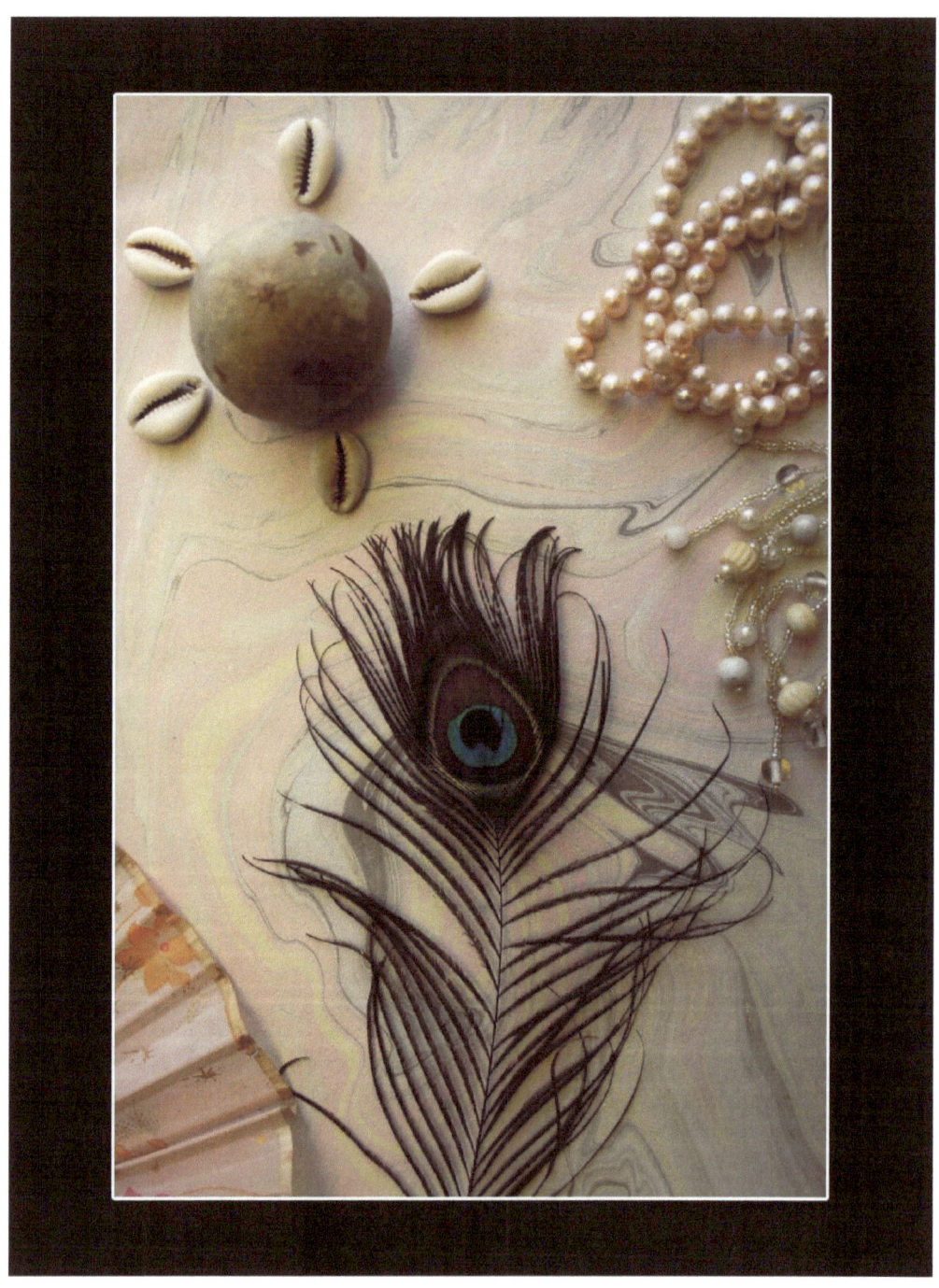

"After Cosmic Slop" 11″x14″ This piece was inspired by the song "Cosmic Slop" by Funkadelic and contains symbols of the Yoruba goddess Osun/Oshun. Hand painted paper, peacock feather, necklace, fan, pearls, cowrie shells, seed, wood, acrylic paint, glass, gold dust. Dimensions: Variable but inside a shadow box. Price: $475.00

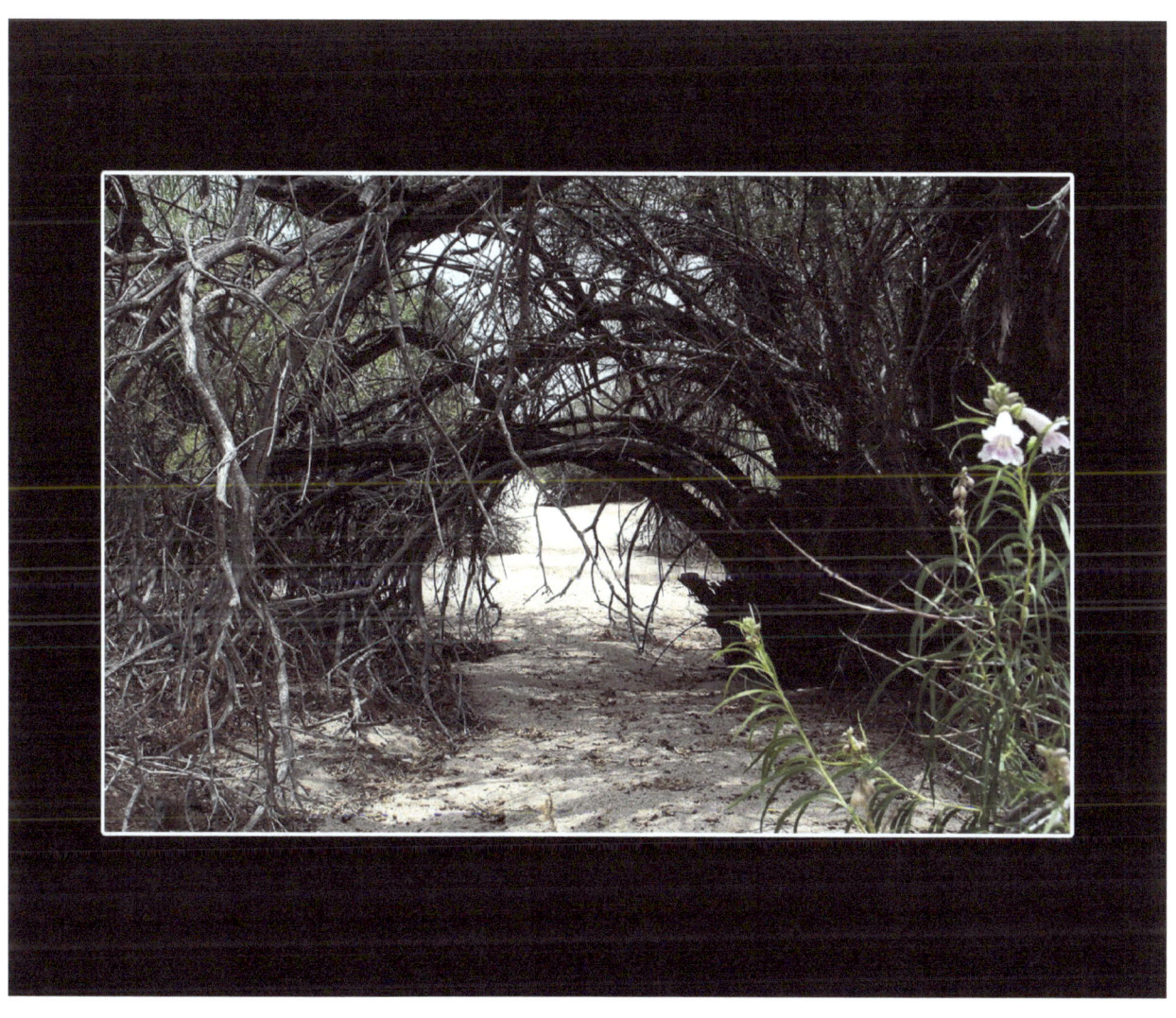

"JT Cove" 8"x10" on 11″x14″ Photograph depicting analogy for life's journey.
Media: Hand printed color photograph. Price: $500.

Ron Witherspoon, MFA
Photographer/Artist
www.RonWitherspoonPhotography.com

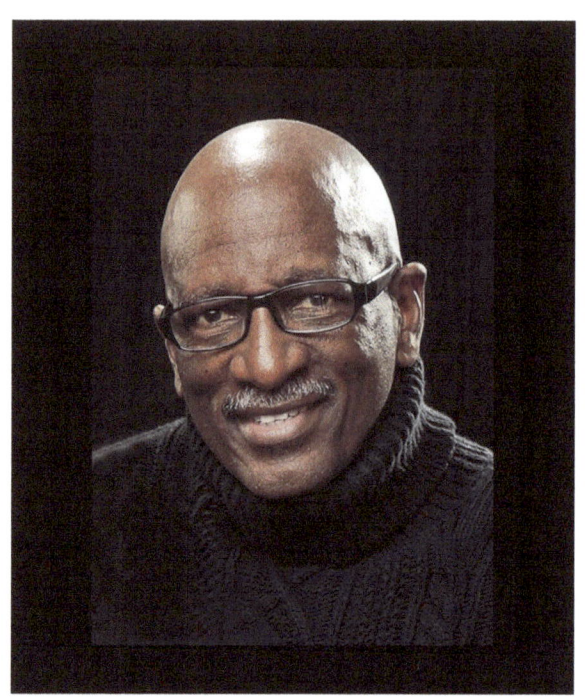

Artist Statement:

"Photography is one form of universal communication. What you see as finished work is the culmination of every facet of your thoughts and experience focused on a window of stimulating opportunity. I am just the conduit for your vicarious experience with my vision. Simply stated, my work should be viewed and bring about an internal reaction – be it negative or positive."

My photography career began with a Kodak Instamatic Camera near my 12th birthday purchased with Blue Chip Stamps. Since then I've earned a Bachelor of Arts in Communications from San Francisco State University, served 6 years in the U.S. Army as a Photojournalist, and earned a Master of Fine Arts in Photography and Digital Imaging from Georgia State University.

I love living life as a photographer!

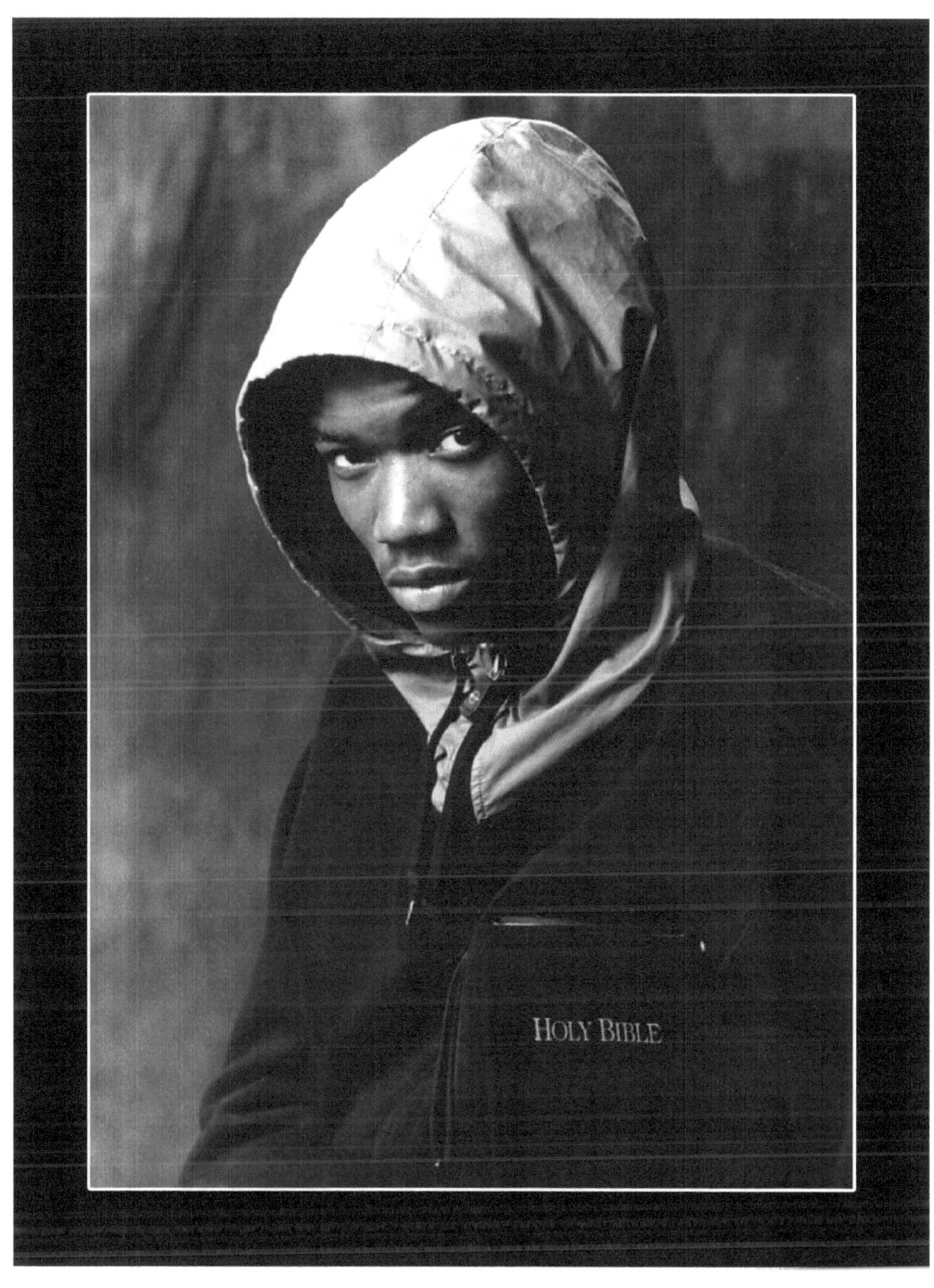

"Hooded Right" 23″W x 27″H   B&W Photograph $ 700.00

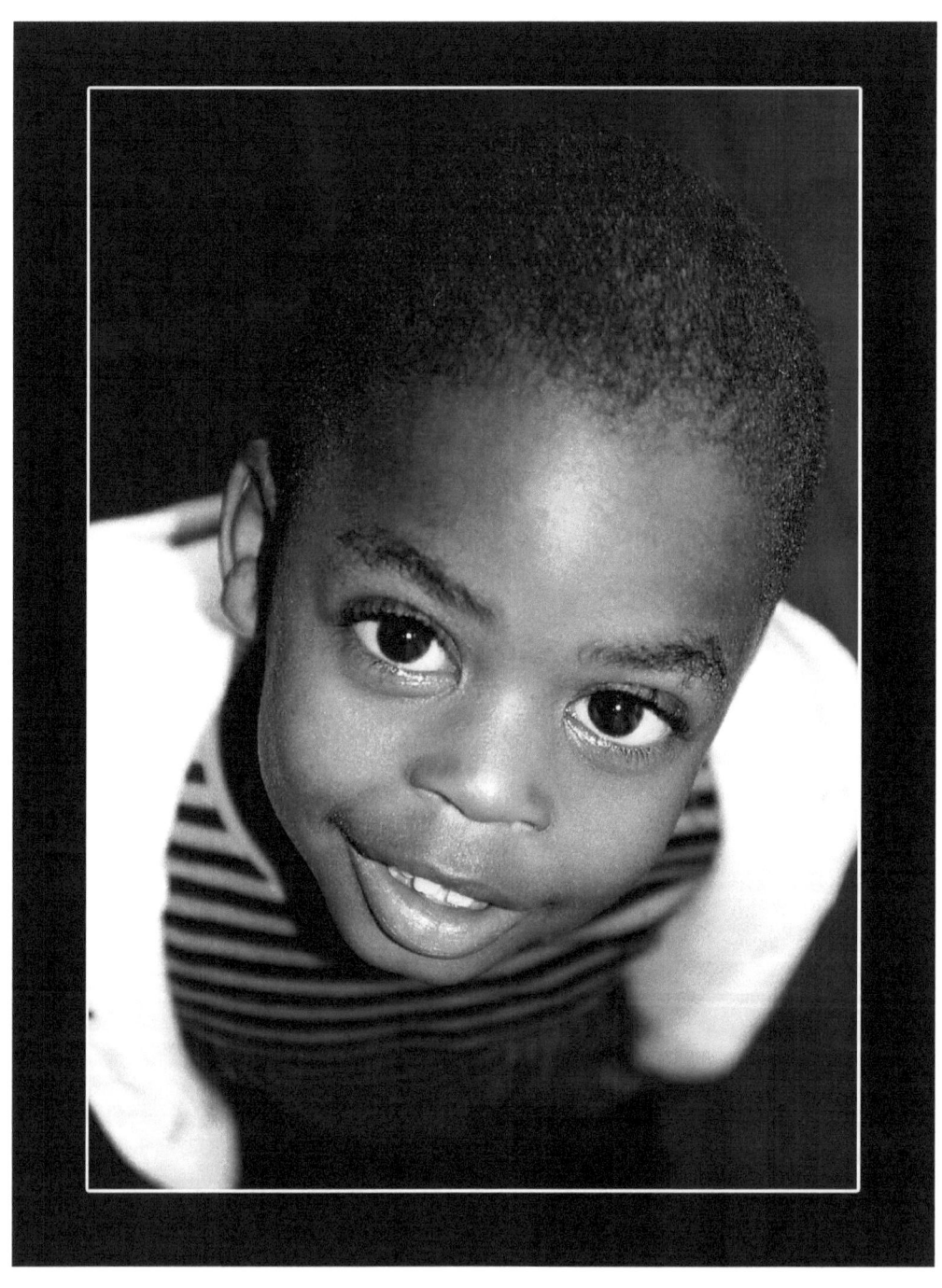

"Innocent Eyes" 23"W x 27"H   B&W Photograph $700.00

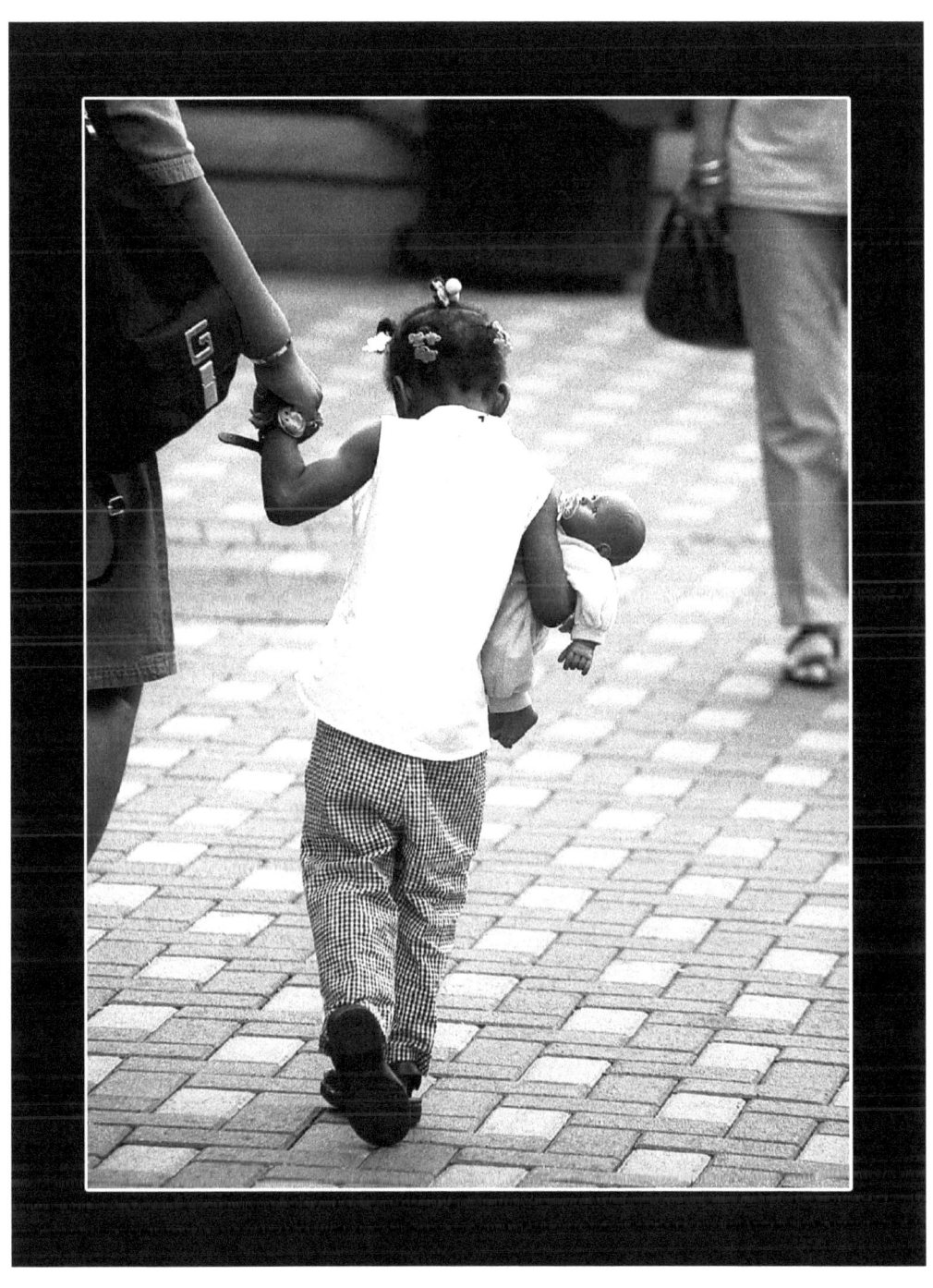

"Nini, Mommie & Me"   23″Wx27″H   B&W Photograph $1,100.00

Katelynn Yhon
Painter/Potter
www.kryartinc.com

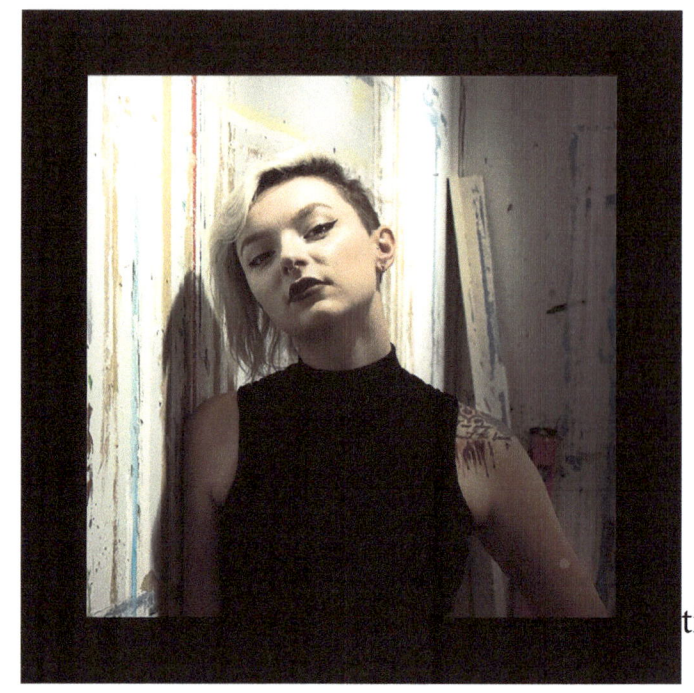

My paintings relate to an inner versus outer experience. I use poetry, drawing and painting, combining them all to create textual image. I also use a certain level of realism and abstraction when working with the human form. My subject matter tends to revolve around the figure: Portraits, bodies, internal organs, eyes, bones, and hands.

I like to look to different graffiti-artists for inspiration. The works of Rae B.K and Jean-Michael Basquiat are particularly inspiring. The way they paint the figure and combine graphic as well as abstract imagery with text is very captivating. I'm also inspired by sure but I like to approach this genre through illustration. Surrealism is interesting in the way that it relates to the subconscious mind and pulls the viewer in due to the odd realism of the style, but I have always loved Illustration and how it can effectively communicate information.

I try to combine surrealistic, abstract, and illustrative ideas into my work. I usually start my work by adding random marks to a canvas. This creates an interesting base to start my process as well as a representation of the subconscious. I like to work with portraiture or anatomy which adds an element of reality into the abstract marks. Then I add text, smooth lines, collage, and or geometric shapes to counter balance the realism. I feel that this gives my work depth and engages the viewer more than just a "normal" portrait or realistic painting.

When painting portraits, I'm inspired by the human experience. While we see people every day, we don't tend to ask ourselves what the person across the room is thinking or what's going on in their life. We're so saturated by people and images of people that we don't stop and think what's going behind the façade. I tend to make my portraits off putting, some bordering on grotesque, to prove a point. We all have faults and flaws and it's ok to recognize these aspects. No one is perfect and we all have secrets and stories. We all have lived lives that are just as intricate and meaningful as the next person.

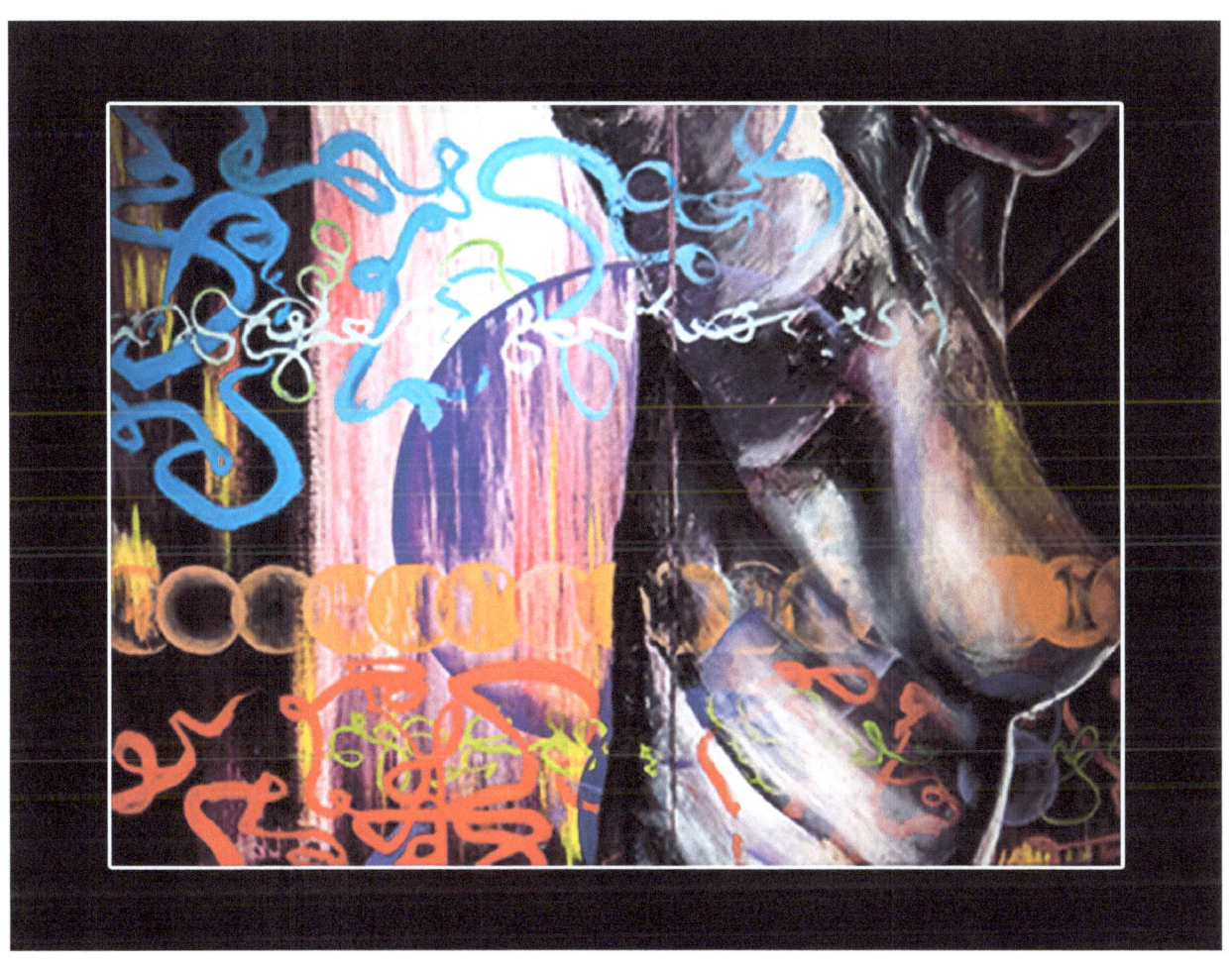

"Figure Study" 20″x30″ Acrylic & Oil on Canvas $500.00

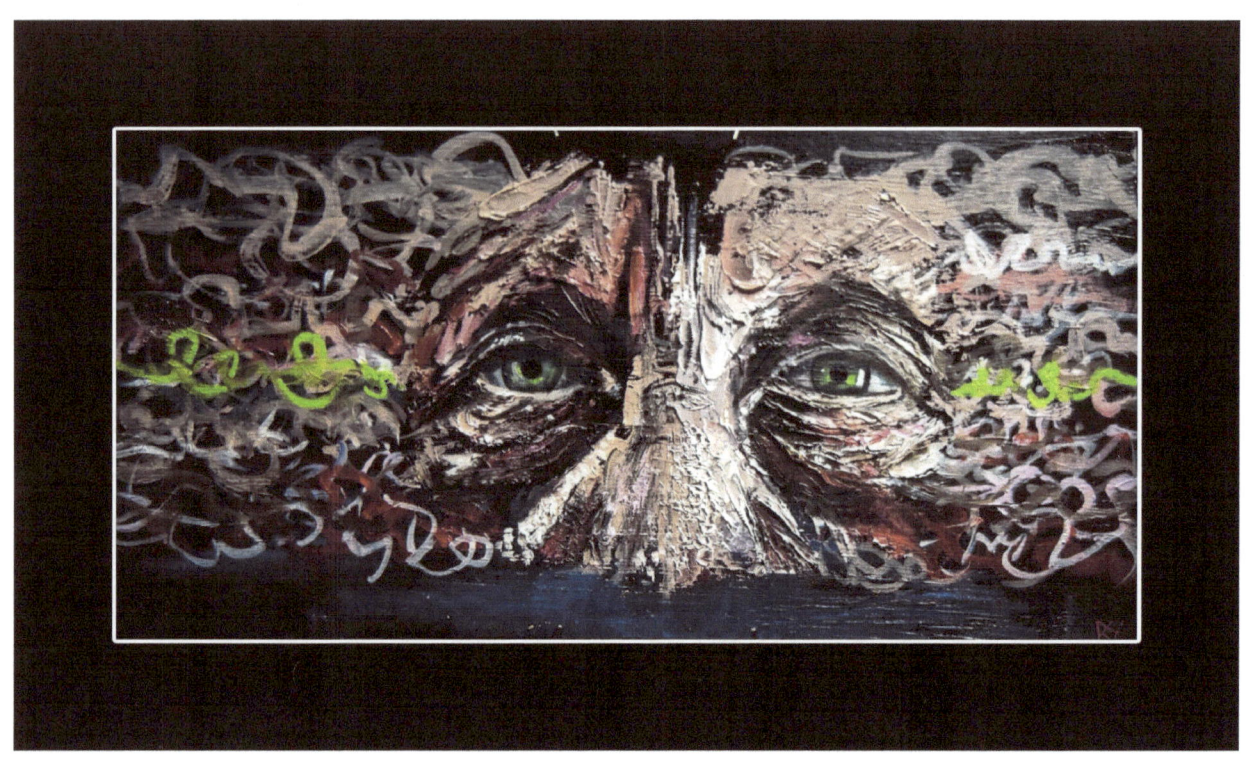

"Sight" 6″x12″   Oil on Wood Panel $150.00

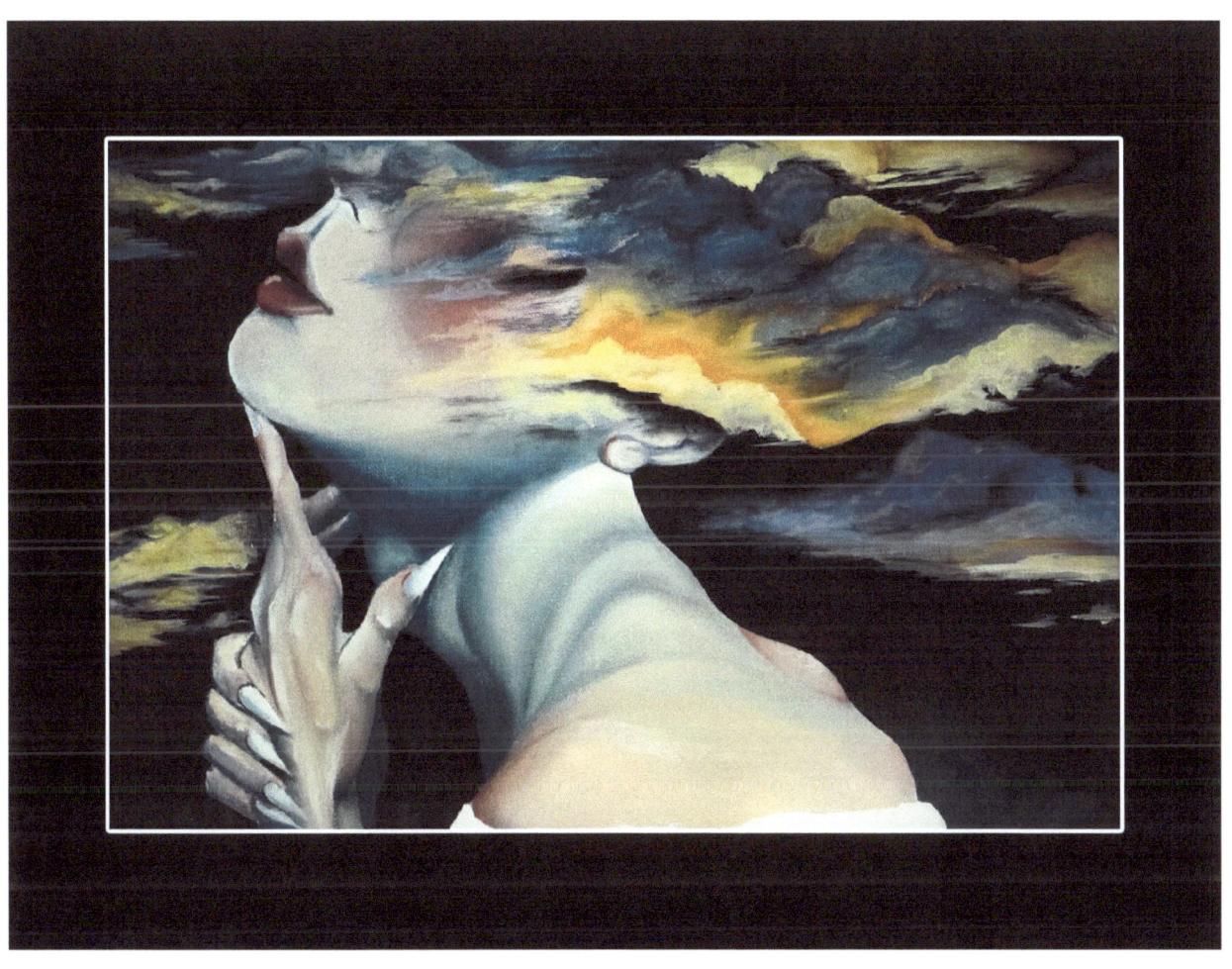

"Head in The Clouds" 16″x20″   Oil on Canvas $350.00

Thanks To All Who Made This Exhibition Possible

Including The Gallery Ambassadors
JEANINE BLANEY * FANTACEE BROWN * BARBARA CAHEE * ANDREW DUMAS
SHEILA FRANKLIN * PENNY GILLESPIE * KAREN HARTFIELD
VERNELL HENDERSON * CHARLENE JEFFERSON *CATHERINE JORDAN
SHAWN LEWIS * HOWARD LINDSEY, Ph.D * JOANN McARTHUR
WILLIAM MAYO * MARC NICHOLS * NICOLE MONCRIEF
JASMINE PATTERSON * PATSY SHELTON *CAROLYNN WHITE
&
CLAUDIA WILLIAMS

"The Ambassadors are a dynamic volunteer group that donates time and other resources to advocate on BHG's behalf throughout the community."

A Special Thanks To All The Artists In The Exhibition

A Special Thanks To
Daphne Taylor Lee
My Editor, 1st Assistant, Muse, Best Friend
&
Wife

www.ingramcontent.com/pod-product-compliance
Lightning Source LLC
Chambersburg PA
CBHW051102180526
45172CB00002B/738